Michel Renouard

Wonderful Finistère

Photographs by Hervé Boulé

BY THE SAME AUTHOR
(selection)

Lumière sur Kerlivit, 1964.

Le Chant des Adieux, 1976 ; 2nd edition 1979.

Châtellerault, Ouest-France, 1986.

Nouveau Guide de Bretagne, Ouest-France, 1988.

A New Guide to Brittany, Ouest-France, 1984.

Art roman en Bretagne, Ouest-France, 1977.

Romanische Kunst in der Bretagne, Ouest-France, 1979.

Romanesque Art in Brittany, Ouest-France, 1980.

La Bretagne, Ouest-France, 1982.

La Bretagna, Ouest-France, 1986.

Die Bretagne, Ouest-France, 1987.

Brittany, Ouest-France, 1984.

Guide du Morbihan, Ouest-France, 1983.

Guide de Bretagne, SECALIB, 1986.

Bretagne (photos by H. Champollion), Ouest-France, 1984.

Bretagne (photos by J.-P. Gisserot), SECALIB, 1986.

Mon premier guide de Bretagne (drawings by C. Lazé), Ouest-France, 1987.

Top : *The harbour at Le Conquet.*

Middle :
A religious procession at Penhors.

Bottom : *Kerouat Mill.*

Front cover :
The harbour at Le Guilvinec.

Back cover : *The Pointe du Van.*

First published in French under the title Aimer le Finistère.

The Cap Sizun Nature Reserve.

For Paul Le Menn

All French people are well aware of a fact that only some dare to set down in black and white - against the background of gold and emerald green that is Armorica, Finistère stands out more than any other area. There is no other French département that offers as many riches as Finistère, a region that is aptly-named and much-loved, the End of the World, a full stop. It was here, for many centuries, that the Western world teetered. And it was from here (for in Brittany, as in India, life is a never-ending succession of fresh starts) that seafarers and adventurers, "tramps and captains", set off for a Western world that was even further away, or for a totally New World.

First of all, the Finistère region is outstanding for its geographical situation. Lying at the confluence of the Atlantic Ocean and the English Channel, it has always been one of the busiest places in the world. All the vessels in History, all the galleons, and all the caravels, their sails filled with offshore winds and the taste of adventure, have passed each other on the seas to the west of this one last peninsula. And at some time in their lives all the old seadogs have wandered the streets of Brest, a port that summarizes the long prodigious adventure of the Finistère region all by itself. The winds have more bite there, the drizzle is more pervasive, and love affairs are more beautiful than elsewhere. Poets, songsters and novelists were quick to recognise this - and very few towns have been sung of more attractively than Brest.

But Finistère is also an abundance of wonderful scenery, as anybody who has ever written a book about Brittany has soon found out. When it comes to selecting illustrations, it is views of Finistère that are chosen two times out of three. For many French people, and even for a large number of Bretons, visiting Brittany means visiting Finistère. And how could it be otherwise ? The most striking landscapes in Armorica are here, along a coastline that stretches over 310 miles, a violent rugged coast running from Le Pouldu to Locquirec. Between these two ports, there are so many varied views that any

3

A marriage of land and sea...

attempt to list them is, by nature, unfair and always incomplete. There are the wide open spaces of the bay in Audierne and the Bigouden region, the rocks at Cap Sizun and the Pointe du Raz, the mysterious bay at Douarnenez, the rough cliffs in Crozon, the rugged country of the abers *(inlets)*, to name but a few. And, as is only right, the islands in Finistère are the best-known islands in Brittany - the Glénans, Sein, Molène, Ushant, and even Batz. There are very few regions anywhere in the world with as maritime a character as Finistère.

Yet the extreme western tip of Brittany has another, quite different

are beginning to tire of rusticity only have to climb a tumulus or hill (there is always one within sight) and they will see in the distance an expanse of blue sea. All things considered, Finistère is first and foremost a marriage of land and sea. And it's a successful marriage, no doubt about that, even if at times it can be sultry, stormy, and squally. The 1987 hurricane, which was exceptional for its violence, proved that nature always has the last word.

The anger of the elements has not spared the third of all Finistère's attractions - its artistic heritage. Most of it, in a region that was "the land of priests", is of a religious nature - churches, chapels, wayside crosses (or calvaries), crucifixes, and Christianised springs. Some of the villages have dozens of sanctuaries, many of them abandoned and condemned to oblivion. Yet this open-air museum is so full of exhibits that they could never all be maintained in good condition. One of the unusual features of Finistère, especially in the north, is its unique collection of parish closes. These monuments are the remains of a period of ardent faith, parish pride... and economic prosperity. Parishes competed with their neighbours, and each community made sure that its earthly existence was marked by the finest tower, the most outstanding calvary, or the most attractive ossuary. No visit to Finistère would be complete without a trip round the parish closes. The best-known are in Saint-Thégonnec, Guimiliau, Lampaul-Guimiliau, Sizun, Commana, Pleyben and La Martyre. Not to mention the cloisters in Daoulas, the abbey at Landévennec, the calvary in Tronoën, the basilica in Le Folgoët, the chapel in Saint-Herbot, the church in Locronan, and the cathedrals in Quimper and Saint-Pol-de-Léon. Or you may prefer humble chapels like the ones in Saint-Jaoua, Saint-They or Notre-Dame du Crann.

Other constructions have also been part and parcel of Man's adventurous history (some of them originally had religious significance but we have lost the key that would enable us to understand them). First and foremost there are the remarkable

facet, one that is just as wild but more rural and more secretive - inland Brittany, a region of forests and uplands (e.g. the Monts d'Arrée and the Montagnes Noires). In summer, the crowds rush to the coast and the beaches. Yet only a few miles from the sea you can always find remote areas, villages cut off from the outside world, hamlets that have probably never been visited by any strangers. Inversely, campers who

A catamaran race off Brest (photo by J.-P. Prével).

prehistoric monuments - dolmens, passage graves, and menhirs. Plouarzel, for example, has the tallest menhir in Brittany (32 ft. high). Plouézoc'h has one of the largest cairns in Europe. Commana and Plouescat have some outstanding passage graves. The alignments in Lagad-Yar near Camaret still comprise some 140 stones. For those who prefer more Cartesian or less ancient monuments, there is ample to satisfy their curiosity. The old streets in Quimper, the town square in Locronan, the old houses in Morlaix or Guerlesquin are all very fine examples of vernacular architecture. Castles and manor-houses are legion, of course, from Kerjean to Trévarez, not forgetting

Kérouzéré or Trémazan. And when visitors are worn out by all these excursions, they can always go to Douarnenez and ask to be told the story of King Gradlon and the sunken town of Ys. Or perhaps they may prefer the Baie des Trépassés - for Finistère is also a land of myths and legends.

Yet how can one ever really get to know a country without knowing its language ? From this point of view, Finistère is the most homogeneous of all the counties in Brittany, as well as being the most "Breton" of all the regions, for the Celtic language is more or less spoken throughout its length and breadth. Finistère is not only a land of seafarers and farmers;

it is also an exceptional breeding ground for teachers, linguists and writers (many of them, in fact, are all three at the same time). Yet this is hardly a paradox because examination successes are the only hope of the poor. Visitors who feel they either cannot or do not wish to learn the Breton language (and this is a mistake on their part) can always make the best of one of the (few) wet days and spend their time reading some of the literary masterpieces translated from the Breton, e.g. Lan Inizan's "La Bataille de Kergidu", Youenn Drezen's "Notre-Dame Bigoudenn", Roparz Hemon's "Le Voyageur de l'hiver" or Pierre Jakez Hélias' "Horse of Pride". Those who prefer French writers will also be able to enjoy some excellent works since Finistère was the birthplace of Henri Queffélec, Michel Mohrt, or Alain Robbe-Grillet. Even avid readers of detective stories will have no difficulty in finding strong grim tales written by sons of Finistère to while away their sleepless nights. This is even one of the county's specialities (Auguste Le Breton, after all, the bard of slang and brawls, was born in Lesneven).

It is difficult to write about Finistère without automatically waxing lyrical. But we shall leave that to aspiring undergraduate poets and invite you, without further ado, to visit the region as the alphabet, or our fancy, takes us.

Wonderful Finistère? For the author, events have turned full circle. It was in July 1957 that he first came to know the county, starting with Pleyben, Sainte-Anne-la-Palud and Douarnenez. A few years later, he called his first novel (now unobtainable) "Kerlivit", after a small village in Argol where he had once pitched his tent! Over the past 30 years, he has gone back to the region time and time again in an effort to learn more about it.

Being fond of a region does not necessarily mean giving way to exaggeration and hyperbole. It means remembering a few precious moments, despite the passage of time. It means writing so that you never quite forget a July shower over the bay in Douarnenez, a particularly intense moment in the church in Commana, a birthday in a house in Le Cloître-Pleyben nestling amidst the trees, and perhaps even a patch of blue sky (the blue of the last few days of childhood) between the pine trees of Kerlivit.

Argol : the parish close. ▶

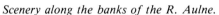

Scenery along the banks of the R. Aulne.

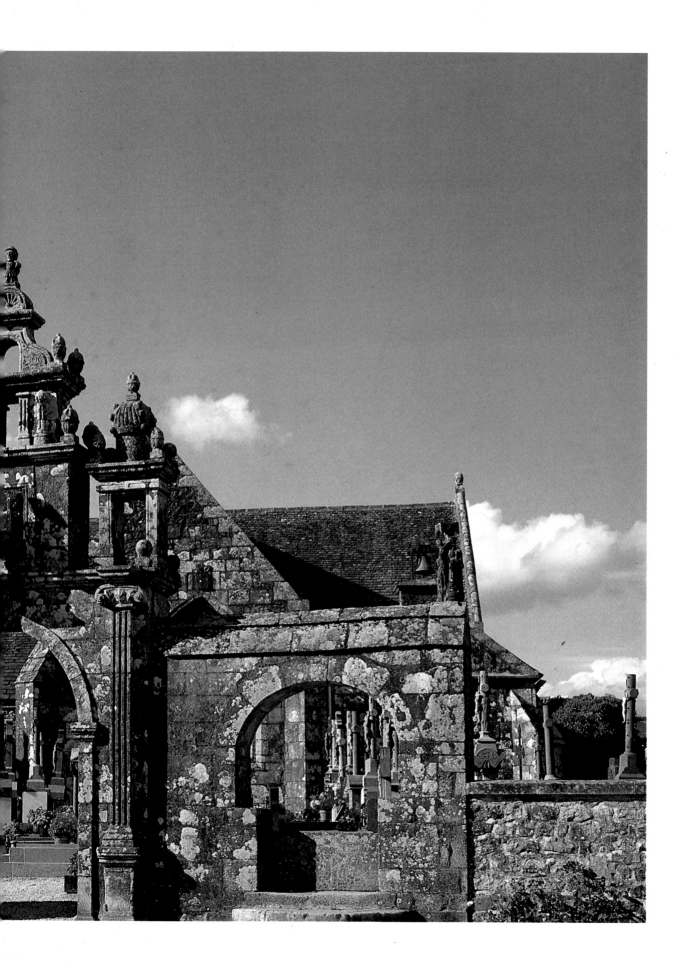

ARGOL

14m. W of Châteaulin

This little village has a particularly fine parish close. On reaching the cemetery, visitors go through a gateway in the form of a triumphal arch (1659) past the statue of King Gradlon. The ossuary dates from the 17th century. The church is older (16th century) but was restored in later centuries.

The north coast is attractive and little known. From the pinewoods of **Kerlivit,** there is a road down to the cove at **Poulmic,** the site of the Lanvéoc-Poulmic **Fleet Air Arm Base.** The Navy has had a training establishment here since 1945.

The village of **Telgruc-sur-Mer** to the south-west of Argol, which was razed to the ground during the war, has been rebuilt.

ARMORICA REGIONAL PARK

The Armorica Park is not fenced in and its boundaries are marked only on maps. It is a "natural" park, formed in 1969 (and stretching from the Monts d'Arrée to Ushant) by 33 small towns and villages in association with the County of Finistère and the town of Brest. Its main objectives are the conservation of everything that can be saved, and increased public awareness through the creation of unusual displays and projects.

The area covers some 75,000 hectares and comprises both country and sea. It is subdivided into four sectors : the Monts d'Arrée (q.v.), which is without doubt the largest sector, the Aulne Estuary (including Ménez-Hom), the tip of the Crozon Peninsula, and the islands of Ushant and Molène. This was the reason for the setting-up of a Centre for Rural Techniques and Traditions in **Saint-Rivoal** in the Monts d'Arrée (20 m. SW of Morlaix).

Other offshoots of the park project are the Museum of Rural Education in **Trégarvan,** the River Centre in the mill at Vergraon in **Sizun,** the Mineral Centre in Saint-Hernot in **Crozon,** and the Hunting Centre in **Scrignac** (cf. Monts d'Arrée and Ushant).

Kerouat : the miller's house. ▶

Ménez-Meur Estate.

The **Ménez-Meur Estate** (423 hectares) lies at Hanvec, some 5 miles from Saint-Rivoal. There are walks and bridlepaths.

It is possible to spot endangered species in the park - wild boar, Ushant sheep, stags etc. On the moors, moufflon can be seen in their natural habitat, while further on beavers work away in a stream. The Kerhouat Mill-Museum in **Commana** was opened in the 1970's. Other projects are underway at the present time.

THE MONTS D'ARREE

At 1,250 ft. **Tuchenn-ar-Gador** (i.e. the Mound of the Throne, rather stupidly taken into French as the Toussaines Peak) is the highest point in the whole of Brittany. It is closely followed by the **Roc'h Trévézel** (1,245 ft.), Mont Saint-Michel de Brasparts (1,238 ft.) and the Roc'h Trédudon (1,196 ft.).

The mountains form a natural geographical feature in which the R.Ellez rises. The deserted, even unreal appearance of this timeless landscape has given the place a special meaning. The bottom of the corrie is formed by **yeun Ellez,** i.e. the Ellez Marshes. They have become a lake whose waters were used, from 1966 to 1985, in the cooling system of a nuclear power station. Yet, in spite of everything, this isolated region has lost none of its inherent strangeness. Will-o'-the-wisps are still to be seen here. Standing guard over the souls of the departed who wander through the marshes is the chapel at the top of the **Mont Saint-Michel de Brasparts.** The Saint-Michel farmstead in the village houses arts and crafts exhibitions.

Notre Dame Church (1485, with later alterations) in **Brennilis** (from ''brenn'' meaning ''a hill'' and ''iliz'', ''a church'') has a traceried belltower over a double doorway.

A quarter of a mile to the north of Brennilis is the **Ti-ar-Boudiked dolmen** (the Fairies' House), which is 45 ft. long and partially covered by a barrow.

Roc'h Trévézel.

◀ *The island of Batz.*

AUDIERNE
3m. SW of Pont-Croix

Audierne is one of those towns and villages whose Breton name is quite unexpected for French speakers - Gwaien. It got its name from the fact that the harbour (the only one of any size in the Sizun Peninsula) nestles in the estuary of the R.Gwain (or Goyen) which flows as far as Pont-Croix. Audierne is not only a fishing port (tuna, shellfish, and especially crayfish); it is also a seaside resort.

From the bridge over the Goyen, there is a general view of the area, with the houses on the harbour's edge backing onto the hills behind. A trip to the **Pointe de Lervily** provides a number of views over the left bank of the ria, the coastline down to Plouhinec, Audierne's beach, and the sea.

Esquibien to the west has a church whose main doorway has been turned into a war memorial (1617, with later restorations). Inside the church is a 15th-century alabaster Pietà.

BANNALEC
20m. E of Quimper

The name Bannalec is of Breton origin and means "land of broom". The **Quimerc'h Manor** (1828) to the east was built atop a conical mound.

Despite its 16th- and 17th-century tower and its extremely rare hinged statue of the Virgin Mary, the church is of little interest, but there are three chapels which are not without charm - the one in **La Véronique** (1604) to the west, **Saint-Cado** (17th but with restoration) to the south-east, and the **Saint-Jacques** (or St. James, 16th century) chapel to the north on the

banks of the R.Isole. The **Kerchuz Mill** (1897, with later restoration) is the last working mill on this river.

To the south-west of La Véronique in Kernével stands **Le Moustoir Chapel,** which has been restored. The portal with its twisted colonnettes (16th century) was based on the one in Saint-Herbot. Further west, the **Holy Trinity Chapel** in Melgven dates partly from the 16th century. It was one of the chapels along the Tro-Breizh route (Tro-Vreizh is more grammatical, it means "Round Brittany"), a 375-mile trip made on foot by the faithful. The pilgrimage passed through Saint-Pol-de-Léon, Quimper, Vannes, Dol, Saint-Malo, Saint-Brieuc and Tréguier and corresponded to the founder saints - Pol, Corentin, Patern, Samson, Malo, Brieuc, and Tugdual. The tradition died out in the 17th century.

ISLAND OF BATZ
Off Roscoff

Located two nautical miles off Roscoff (15 mins. away by boat), the island stretches over 2 1/2 miles from west to east and is approximately half-a-mile wide. Although it is low-lying, it protects Roscoff from the north winds. The south coast has a particularly mild climate and early vegetables are grown there. The islanders also make a living from sea-weed (for many years the only source of fuel on this treeless island), fishing and tourism. To the south-east is an overgrown **Colonial Garden** and, nearby, the ruins of a **Romanesque chapel** (10th century) once part of a monastery founded by St. Pol Auré-lien. In the same area, there is also a prehistoric graveyard and dolmen (made Christian in the 13th century by the addition of a calvary). The north coast is wilder but, some say, even more attractive.

◀ *The harbour at Audierne.*

There are fine walks on the island. To the west you can visit the light-house (211 steps) built at the highest point along the coastline (114 ft.).

BENODET
9m. S of Quimper

In Breton, the name of this yacht-ing marina is an indication of its geographical position at the mouth of the R.Odet. A cosmopolitan atmosphere has reigned here for many years. It was, in fact, the Bri-tish who first discovered the resort and they continue to come back in large numbers. In summer, the popu-lation rises from 2,500 to 35,000.

Between Bénodet Point and **Mous-terlin**, the **Mer Blanche** (White Sea) is a peaceful lagoon, the haunt of onshore fishermen and poets in search of inspiration.

To the east on the Fouesnant road, the late 11th-century **Chapel of St. Brigitte of Perguet** has a Roman-esque nave. The 16th-century chancel

The Chapel of St.Bridget of Perguet.

and transept are separated from the nave by a 12th-century ribbed vault.

To the north-east lies the church in **Clohars-Fouesnant,** which is mainly 15th and 16th centuries. The south side is preceded by a lodge containing archives. The church itself has a sculpture of the Holy Trinity (15th century). Between Clohars and Pleuven stands the 18th-century **Cheffontaines Castle** ; nearby are the ruins of another, older castle. To the west is the spring in **Le Drennec** (16th century) which has a Pietà and a calvary. See also Fouesnant.

On the right bank of the Odet opposite Bénodet is **Sainte-Marine,** a summer holiday resort. In olden days, St. Moran was worshipped there. He was an Irishman who, thanks to the genius of rather absent-minded translators, changed sex and became St. Marine ! Emile Zola was a guest in **Kerbirinic Castle** on the banks of the Odet. The road south leads to the **Pointe de Combrit.**

The Odet Valley.

BERVEN
11m. E of Lesneven, in Plouzévédé

For centuries, Berven has been a place of pilgrimage because of its **chapel,** Notre-Dame (15th and more especially 16th centuries), which is of great interest to architectural buffs. Its lantern-dome (1576) is said to have been the first of its kind in Brittany. Its close is famous for its triple-arched **triumphal gateway** similar to the one in Sizun. Inside the church, the most remarkable features are the reredos, a rood screen dating from 1720, and a Rod of Jesse showing a marked Rhenish influence (late 16th century). The choir screen is also worthy of note.

To the north of Berven lie the ruins of **Kergournadeac'h Castle** ("The abode of the man who does not run away") dating from 1605. The corner towers and chimneys are particularly impressive.

BODILIS
16m. W of Morlaix

Bodilis is said to mean "the thicket round the church" (but in Old Breton, "bod" meant "a place of residence" or "a refuge"). Whether real or imaginary, the thicket has disappeared but the chapel is still there. It dates mainly from 1564-1670. The large south porch (late 16th century) was built in the Classical Renaissance style and was one of the first of its kind in Brittany.

Plounéventer to the west was the site of a Gallo-Roman town. **Mésarnou Manor** was built in the early 16th century but is now in a very poor state of repair.

In **Saint-Servais** to the south-west, there is a close with a 16th-century ossuary. Nearby, on the banks of the R.Elorn, **Brézal Mill** (with its Flamboyant Gothic doorway) is a pleasant place for a stroll. Not far away stands the chapel of Pont-Christ (cf. La Roche-Maurice).

Sainte-Marine. ▶

◀ *The Pietà in Brasparts.*

Brest : the Tanguy Tower.

BRASPARTS
27m. N of Quimper

Brasparts has a 16th-century church close. On the **ossuary,** there are not one but two statues of Ankou (Death). The **calvary** has a striking Pietà on which three figures hold the body of Christ. St. Michael is also represented, fighting a dragon. The apostles stand guard in the **church porch** (1590) topped by lantern turrets. And it is quite likely that theirs is no easy task for the consoles are swarming with terrifying monsters including one particularly grotesque figure with horns and a snake's tail, holding an apple in his right hand. **Inside** the church, note the Passion Window (16th century), the Pietà, and the 17th-century Rosary reredos.

BREST
48m. N of Quimper

Brest stands on a quite exceptional spot. Built on a plateau, the town overlooks the huge natural harbour which can take the largest ships and even atomic submarines. Accessible only by a narrow strait (1 1/2 m. at its widest point), it is easy to defend. This explains Brest's rôle as a military and maritime base for approximately 2,000 years (the Romans built mighty fortifcations here). It also explains why, during the Second World War, the Allies' planes pounded away at the naval base until it was totally destroyed.

There is almost nothing left of the old town. The **castle** houses the Regional Shipping Office while the **Tanguy Tower** (16th century but much restored) is now a museum. A 17th-century gateway stands in the middle of the modern Square du Commandant l'Herminier.

With the opening of the **arsenal** c. 1631 came a group of professional sculptors who were to exercise considerable influence on the artistic life of the region. From 1750-1852, Brest was famous for its penitentiary. When a convict escaped, a blank shot was fired to warn the population. Hence, apparently, the popular expression "tonnerre de Brest" ("Brest thunder").

Modern town planning enthusiasts will find much to interest them in Brest - blocks of flats and offices, wide avenues, huge squares, a vertical lift-bridge (the Recouvrance is the largest of its kind in Europe), St. Louis' Church (1958), and the Arts and Cultural Centre (1969) which was almost completely destroyed by fire on 26th November 1981.

As to shipping enthusiasts, they cannot but be fascinated by the view from the Cours Dajot or the Boulevard de la Marine (beyond the **Rue de Siam** which is named after a group of diplomats who visited Brest in 1685). At the end of the Penfeld Estuary, there is the dockyard with its navy vessels, tugs, torpedo boats, refit basins, jetties and gigantic cranes. But the finest view is from the Corniche road (beyond the Recouvrance Bridge). Laninon Harbour takes the largest ships; it is outlined against the background of the main harbour and nearby, depending on the weather, you might see the Crozon Peninsula, the Ile Longue, and the Pointe des Espagnols.

CAMARET-SUR-MER
26m. NW of Châteaulin

For many years, Camaret was France's main crayfish harbour but between 1955 and 1981 the fleet dwindled from 42 to 5. Because of its geographical situation near Brest and its strategic position, it has undergone attacks on many occasions over the centuries. In July 1694, the Anglo-Dutch army was pushed back into the sea by Vauban, but some 1,200 men lost their lives in the fighting. And it was here in August 1801 that the American Robert Fulton carried out the first trials with his submarine.

In the late 19th and early 20th centuries, Camaret was a popular haunt of artists such as Eugène Boudin, André Antoine and Henry Bernstein. The Provençal poet Saint-Pol-Roux (1861-1940) spent the latter years of his life here, in a Neogothic **manor** that now lies in ruins, on the road to Pen-Hir.

On the shore in Camaret stands the **Chapel of Rocamadour** (the origin of its name is a mystery) which was carefully rebuilt with great attention to detail after a fire in 1910. **Vauban Castle** (1689-1695), a sort of small defensive fort, is unique in French architecture. It now houses a naval museum.

The **Pointe de Toulinguet** is a highly-coloured mixture of rocks, caves, beach and cliffs. On the road to Pen-Hir are the **Lagad-Yar** (or "chicken's eye") **standing stones.** There are now only 143 stones left out of the 700 that stood on this spot in the late 18th century.

The **Pointe de Pen-Hir,** a terrifying spur of rock 227 ft. high jutting out into the sea, is the most impressive beauty spot in Brittany. It is extended by four enormous outcrops call the **Tas-de-Pois.**

From Camaret to the **Pointe des Espagnols** (Spaniards' Point), the road runs between Ministry of Defence establishments.

Camaret.

Camaret : the Vauban fortress. ▲

The Tas-de-Pois rocks. ▼

◄ *Pointe de Pen-Hir.*

CARANTEC
9m. NW of Morlaix

Approaching Carantec on the coast road from Morlaix on a day of spring tides and sunshine is an unforgettable experience.

Before reaching the village, there is a road off the right to **Pen-al-Lann**; it leads to the tip of the peninsula bearing the same name. The pine woods are becoming increasingly scarce as more and more new housing estates are built, but a public park has been laid out in woods on the south side of the hill. Near the headland, a tree-shaded path runs up to the clifftop. From there, there is a panoramic view out to sea - first **Louët Island** with its coastal station, then the **Château du Taureau** built on a reef between 1543 and 1588.

Further out, opposite the Pointe de Barnénez, the **Ile Noire** (lighthouse) and reefs break the surface of the water at low tide, when it is possible to reach the beaches that skirt the peninsula. Northwards, there are several tiny islands, all part of a bird sanctuary.

The main square in Carantec is dominated by the late 19th-century church. The remains of the main door of an older church are also visible. Go round the church and down the road behind it - there are views over the bay of Morlaix. The road leads to **Le Kelenn Beach** (''holly beach'' ?). Then return to the village by taking the first turning on the right signposted **La Chaise du Curé** (Priest's Chair) which is approx. 300 yds. further on. This leads to a promontory overlooking both the Baie de Morlaix and the Penzé Estuary to the west.

The Ile Louët and the Château du Taureau.

Carhaix: St.Trémeur's Church.

CARHAIX-PLOUGUER

29m. SE of Morlaix

Everything seems to point to Carhaix being the capital of the Osmismens in Gallo-Roman times when it was known as Vorgium. It was, in fact, the major road junction in the west of Brittany (ten main roads met at this point). Although there are very few Gallo-Roman remains in the area, Carhaix has provided experts with a large number of objects (many of which are displayed in the museum in Quimper) and coins dating from the 1st-4th centuries.

The long mediaeval period is shrouded in legend. In the 6th century, for example, Carhaix was the residence of Comorre, Count of Poher, the first Breton Bluebeard.

On the **Place du Champ-de-Bataille** to the east stands a statue of La Tour d'Auvergne (1841) by Charles Marochetti, with fanciful bas-reliefs illustrating scenes from the life of Carhaix' most famous son, Théophile-Malo Corret, alias La Tour d'Auvergne, who was passionately interested in two things - the Breton language and warmongering.

The former **collegiate church of St. Trémeur** to the north-west is actually fairly modern (1800-1887) but its porch-belltower dates from 1529-1535. In a central niche on the tympanum above the main door, there is a statue of St. Trémeur holding his head in his hands. Inside, in the north transept, there is a fine statue of Our Lady of Pity. **St. Peter's Church** to the north-west has also been rebuilt and restored over the centuries (especially after the fire of 1923), but it has retained some parts of the 11th-century building (three Romanesque windows on the left of the nave).

Cast : the St. Hubert's Hunt.

Châteaulin : Notre-Dame Chapel. ▶

CAST
4m. SW of Châteaulin

The door of **St. Jerome's Church** dates from the 16th century while other parts of the church are 18th-century. The **calvary** (1660) has a single cross (with Our Lady of Pity and St. Tinidic). In front of the church on a pedestal is a strange monument built of kersantite ; it is known as **St. Hubert's Hunt** (c.1525). The saint, dressed in the costume of Henri II's day, is accompanied by an equerry and two dogs.

CHATEAULIN
17m. N of Quimper

The Cité-sur-Aulne, as it was once called, lies on one of the meanders of the longest river in Finistère (R.Aulne, 90 miles long). It is still a pleasant place for a stroll, along the tree-lined river bank. Water plays an important part in the life of a town that is the capital of Brittany's salmon-fishing industry.

St.Idunet's Church (1867) contains several 18th-century reredos, but the church that visitors should be sure not to miss is **Notre-Dame** (15th and 16th centuries with later restoration) which overlooks the town from a picturesque spot on top of an outcrop of rock.

Port-Launay to the north-east played a part in local history in the 17th century. Nostalgics can stroll along a flower-lined jetty some 750 yds. long.

Nearby, in the village of Saint-Segal to the west, **St. Sebastian's Chapel** (16th-17th centuries) with its mid 16th-century calvary and triumphal gate, is a marvel of subtlety lost in the middle of the countryside.

Saint-Coulitz to the east of Châteaulin has a close with a 16th-century ossuary and a church dating from the 16th and 17th centuries. St.Coulitz taught St.Bridget, one of the patron saints of Ireland.

CHATEAUNEUF-DU-FAOU
22m. NE of Quimper

Lying on the banks of the Aulne at the foot of the Montagnes Noires, Châteauneuf-du-Faou is in a privileged and admirable setting on a hilltop (432 ft.). It is also worth going for a walk along the towpath of the **Nantes-Brest Canal** to the south.

The town has long been dedicated to the Virgin Mary, as shown by the statue of Our Lady of Deliverance in the 19th-century parish church (18th-century tower). The font was decorated by Paul Sérusier (1865-1927), a friend of Gauguin. They first met in Pont-Aven.

The **Chapel of Notre-Dame-des-Portes** to the east on the Laz road is also modern (1880) but it has a Gothic porch (15th century) which was retained from the previous church on this site.

Commana : the passage grave at Mougau-Vian.

Concarneau. ▲

The "Fishermen's Madonna". ▶

COMMANA
9m. SW of Morlaix

Commana, which stands on a barren hill not far from Le Roc'h Trévezel, was once the capital of the "pilhaouerien" i.e. the rag-and-bone men who worked throughout Brittany (it is probably because of them that a duster is sometimes called "pilho" in Upper Brittany). This rather unusual claim to fame did not stop the town from erecting an impressive parish close.

The heavy gateway to the cemetery is decorated with lantern turrets, like the sacristy (1701) in the south-eastern corner. The ossuary-chapel dates from 1686. The **church** (16th-17th century) has a square bell-tower with a stone spire (1592). The

south porch (c.1650) is a fine example of Breton Renaissance architecture.

The church houses the **St. Anne Reredos** (1682) showing the saint with the Virgin Mary and Jesus. Baroque enthusiasts consider it to be one of the finest altar screens in the Léon region. To the right is the Reredos of the Five Wounds. Apart from the statues, the canopy above the font borne by five women representing the Christian virtues is also worthy of note.

One mile to the south-west stands the **Mougau-Vian passage grave.** Legend has it that giants lie buried beneath this 45-foot table comprising five slabs resting on 28 pillars. Engravings can be made out on some of the blocks of stone.

Saint-Sauveur, 4m. to the north-west (the village is called An Drev-Nevez in Breton) has a Renaissance church.

CONCARNEAU
14m. SE of Quimper

In Breton, Concarneau is called Konk-Kernev, i.e. "the creek of Cornouaille" as opposed to Le Conquet or Konk-Léon, the "creek of Léon". The word "Konk" is said to come from the Latin *concha* meaning "a shell" and, by extension, "a basin, creek, or bay" (cf. Conques in the SW French county of Aveyron, and Cancale which was originally known as Konk-Aven, then Konk-Gall). Concarneau is France's foremost tuna fish port. Since 1905, the town has been staging the **Blue Nets Fes-**

Concarneau : the Fishery Museum.

Concarneau : the walled town. ▲
Concarneau : the harbour. ▶

tival every year at the end of August. It is one of the most popular events in Brittany.

In the centuries when Brittany was being evangelised, a priory depending on Landévennec Abbey was founded on the island that is now the walled town. A ring of fortifications was first built in the 13th-14th centuries, rebuilt from 1451-1477, and finally repaired and completed by Vauban in the 17th century.

The **Walled Town** should be seen from the outside, from the Place Jean-Jaurès for example. The ramparts run round an island some 400 yds. long. To the left is a belfry and clocktower which fit in well with the other buildings. The way into the walled town takes visitors through the first set of fortifications to an inner square, then through a second gateway. The **Fishery Museum** is housed in the former prison in the Rue Vauban. You might also like to visit the **Shell Museum**. On the left, beyond the Place Saint-Guénolé, is the Wine Gateway, so-called because boats used to tie up there to unload their cargoes of beverages. At the end of the street on the site of the former castle, there is an open-air theatre. Visitors will get a variety of interesting views of the harbour and town as they walk round the ramparts.

Outside the walled town, the marine biology laboratory of the Collège de France on the seafront houses a **Marinarium** which is open to the public. At the other end of the Boulevard Bougainville is the Sables-Blancs beach from where there are some delightful views out over the Baie de la Forêt.

Keriolet Castle to the north was bought by a Russian princess in the 19th century and rebuilt in the Neo-gothic style by Joseph Bigot c.1865. It was lived in by Prince Yusupov, the murderer of Rasputine.

The harbour at Le Conquet and the Kermorvan Peninsula.

The Crozon Peninsula near Pen-Hir. ▶

LE CONQUET
15m. W of Brest

This small fishing port (specialising in lobster and crayfish) situated on a desolate spot on the westernmost tip of Brittany attracts a large number of tourists because of its two fine beaches - Le Conquet Beach itself (with its enormous rocks) and the Blancs-Sablons, or White Sands, Beach which stretches for a mile along the coast. The name of Le Conquet is well-known to sailors for its **radio coastguard station** on the Pointe Sainte-Barbe.

There are no very old buildings in Le Conquet, for the town was burnt down by the English in 1558. Only a few houses (the ones belonging to British people) were spared.

The church is a fairly recent building (1856) but it contains a 16th-century Passion Window, some 15th-century carvings and the tomb of Mikaël Le Nobletz who came to convert the locals in the 17th century. Until then, they had resisted all attempts to bring them to Christianity (cf. Plouguerneau).

There is a wonderful view from the tip of **Kermorvan Peninsula** to the N. The Ilette Fort is clearly visible standing on what is, at least at high tide, a tiny island. The village of **Trébabu,** nestling in a valley, surprises visitors because of its many mills and lakes.

CROZON PENINSULA
W of Châteaulin

The Crozon Peninsula has an exceptionally large number of grandiose beauty spots in a comparatively small area. The trident jutting out into the Atlantic Ocean between Brest Water to the north and the Baie de Douarnenez to the south is a succession of striking landscapes of cliffs, creeks and rocks worn away into strange shapes by the waves. If you are looking for the secretive, untamed side of Brittany, this may well be the place to find it.

Yet some of Crozon's scenery is closed to the public. To the north beyond Rostellec, **Ile Longue** (''Long Island'' - but it is really a

The "Château" de Dinan.

◀ Pointe de Pen-Hir.

peninsula) belongs to the Navy; it is France's nuclear submarine base. It also has other military establishments. The tiny port of Fret lies at the south-eastern tip of Ile Longue.

The modern church in Crozon (Kraozon, in Breton) has an altarpiece known as the **Reredos of the 10,000 Martyrs.** The highly-coloured fresco features some 400 characters and it was erected in memory of the Theban Legion slaughtered for its faith on Mount Ararat. This remarkable work of art dates from 1624. Although the actor Louis Jouvet (1887-1951) first saw the light of day in Crozon, he was Breton only by an accident of birth.

Morgat to the south is a seaside resort made famous by the artists Maxime Maufra and Henri Rivière. The philosopher Alain wrote his "Entrevues au bord de la Mer" here. A boat trip to the **Morgat Caves** along the cliffs is a pleasant outing. The "gateway" or **Pointe de la Chaise** (Beg-ar-Gador) to the southeast is a picturesque spot. Beyond it are the headlands called Saint-Hernot (cf. Armorica Park), Dolmen and Rostudel.

The D.225 road leads to the **Cap de la Chèvre** (Beg-ar-C'havr, or Goat's Cape), a mighty sandstone headland with cliffs indented by caves. As far as the goat in the cape's name is concerned, it is somewhat of a misnomer. It should be a stag, an animal present in many a legend. Between this headland and the Pointe de Dinan are the most attractive landscapes and seaviews in the peninsula, successions of cliffs, coves, creeks, beaches and capes. The beach at **Lost-Marc'h** (the Breton word for the plant known as mare's tail) is especially charming. Further north, the **"Château" de Dinan** and its headland are connected by two natural archways. Nearby, the **Grottes des Korrigans** (Fairy Grottoes) are remarkable for their colours and their high roofs, but they are difficult to get to. Visitors should not attempt to go there without a guide.

DAOULAS
13m. SE of Brest

Visitors to the remarkable parish close in Daoulas (for the controversy surrounding its name, see Laz) pass through a **porch** dating from 1566. Its amazing topknot is a 19th-century whimsy. Building work on the austere **church** (once a minster) began in 1167 on the remains of a much older abbey. The church was altered on several occasions and underwent major restoration, in the Romanesque style, in 1877 when some of its monuments were displaced and resited elsewhere. The main parts of the building dating from the 12th century are the west front, the north aisle and the seven-arched nave.

The **cloisters** (c.1170) were rebuilt and completed during the 19th-century restoration (which means that some sections are, in fact, reproductions). It is an exceptional example of Romanesque architecture as it was in Brittany at that time (second half of the 12th century) with its colonnettes and magnificent kersantite capitals. In the centre, an octagonal **wash-basin** is richly decorated with geometric patterns; it seems to be of Norman inspiration. At the east end of the cloisters is the wall of the chapter house with its two Romanesque windows.

Further down the hill stands **St.Anne's Chapel** (1667) with its Renaissance doorway. Inside, note the St.Anne and the Virgin Mary Reredos and the polychrome Pietà. Daoulas was an Augustinian monastery from the 12th to the late 18th century; today, it is occupied by Franciscan nuns.

DIRINON
4m. SW of Landerneau

The **parish close** contains a calvary, an ossuary and a church built in the Breton Renaissance style (late 16th and early 17th centuries, extended in the 18th century). Its bell-tower has two bell chambers flanked by balustrades and pilasters decorated with a range of motifs. It also has a spire decorated with four bell turrets. Inside the church, there are some fine **paintings on wood** (c.1720).

To the south is the shrine of St. Nonne, **St.Nonne's fountain** (1623) and, further on, the chapel and fountain of St.Divi, the saint's son.

To the north of Dirinon near **Raoul Lake** is a manorhouse (15th-16th cent.), a mill (1622) and the ruins of St.Aubin's Chapel (1695).

The cloisters in Daoulas.

The harbour at Douarnenez.

◄ *Ploaré Church.*   *Douarnenez: general view of the harbour.* ►

DOUARNENEZ
14m. N of Quimper

Douarnenez is synonymous with the legend of the town of Ys which has been casting a net over its history for centuries past. It has even affected the place-name and nobody is sure of the origin of the word Douarnenez. It would be tempting to think that "douar" is the Breton word for "land" but what, then, would be the meaning of the incomprehensible "nenez"? The most attractive proposition (but probably the least plausible) is that "nenez" comes from "nevez" meaning "new". Douarnenez, says the legend, is a "new land" for it was built after the town of Ys had sunk beneath the waves. And the enchanting Baie de Douarnenez (everybody is at least agreed on this) really was the site of the town of Ys, capital of King Gradlon of Cornouaille.

Unfortunately Gradlon had a daughter, the beautiful Ahès, or Dahud, whose lifestyle was not exactly of the most virtuous kind. And the population followed her deplorable example - much to the displeasure of St.Winwaloe (or Guénolé) who, in his abbey in Landévennec, almost had a heart attack every time he heard tell of the fair Dahud's antics. In His anger, God decided that enough was enough, and He handed the town over to the Devil. Of course, the inevitable happened. The Devil seduced Dahud, forced her to go and fetch the keys to the sluice-gates and, a few moments later, water poured through the town.

But enough of History and Legend intermingled. Let us not forget that Douarnenez is now France's 5th-largest fishing port. **Rosmeur Harbour** to the east should be seen when the boats are coming back, or early in the morning when the fish market is in full swing.

Tréboul to the west has been part of Douarnenez since 1945. A viaduct connects the two parts of the town. To the west of Tréboul is the 162-foot Pointe de Leydé standing high above a pile of rocks lashed by the sea.

A walk along the **Ploumarc'h Path** to the south of Rosmeur Harbour is particularly charming. It leads down to Le Ris Beach and to Ploaré. The whole area has a wealth of **Gallo-Roman remains.**

Ploaré Church (16th century, with 17th-century alterations) is topped by the most impressive belltower (179 ft. high) built in Lower Cornouaille after 1550.

Pouldavid Church to the south is famous for its painted wood panelling (mid 16th-century) and its carillon drum. "Pouldavi" canvas once enjoyed a very high reputation.

The basilica in Le Folgoët.

Le Folgoët : general view of the basilica. ▶

LE FOLGOET
15m. NE of Brest

Le Folgoët Basilica lies one mile south of Lesneven. It has been a famous place of pilgrimage since the 15th century and is one of the finest Flamboyant Gothic churches in the whole of Brittany.

Le Folgoët (literally, "the madman of the woods") was one Salaün or Solomon, a simple-minded creature who was the butt of many a jibe. He lived alone in the woods, endlessly repeating "Ave Maria" or "O Itroun Gwerc'hez Mari" ("Our Lady Virgin Mary"). He slept outdoors, bathed in a fountain, and lived on charity. After his death (c.1358), a lily blossomed on his grave, a lily whose roots, when uncovered, were shown to be growing in Salaün's mouth. The plant bore the inscription "Ave Maria". The local people marvelled at the miracle and came in large numbers to honour Salaün's grave. A short time later,

the Bretons built a basilica.

That, at least, is the legend. A few facts will perhaps serve to show the story in a different light. In 1364, during the War of Breton Succession, Jean de Montfort (who was an adversary of the Blois faction and an ally of the French with Du Guesclin) made a vow that, if he won the Battle of Auray, he would build a basilica to the Virgin Mary. Montfort in fact already enjoyed considerable prestige in the south of Brittany ; after his victory, the new Duke tried to gain recognition in the north. The story of Salaün was a godsend.

The **basilica** was not to be completed until the 15th century, by Jean IV's son, Jean V, whose statue decorates the façade. This was the most prosperous period in the history of independent Brittany. On the outside of the basilica, note the North Tower. It is the only one to have been completed and is reminiscent of the ones on St.Peter's Church in Caen.

LA FORET-FOUESNANT
10m. SE of Quimper

The early 16th-century church has a traditional Cornouaille belltower and steeple. The baptistry, built in 1628 and composed of an enclosure with a carved wooden canopy, surrounds the font. The piscina and basin are a single piece. In addition to the High Altar dating from 1639, note the Rosary painting (17th century) and the 17th- and 18th-century statues (including a Pietà).

The **Château du Stang,** a mile to the north, was built in the 16th century but underwent alteration in the 18th.

A road runs down to the cove opposite the yacht basin at **Port-La-Forêt.**

The Cornouaille Golf Course is a green sward on the eastern side of the bay. Between La Forêt and Concarneau, the banks of the **Anse Saint-Laurent** are covered in woodland that is sure to delight nature lovers.

FOUESNANT
10m. SE of Quimper

Fouesnant looks more like a large village than a real town. Everything contributes to this illusion, including the surrounding countryside with its chestnut trees and apple and cherry orchards. Fouesnant produces the best-known cider in Brittany but this charming region is also the ideal place to see the "giz Foen", i.e. the traditional costume of Fouesnant. You will see a few people wearing it, of course, on a Sunday when church comes out, but there are many more at the Apple-Tree Festival (on the first Sunday after 14th July) or the St. Anne Procession (26th July).

The 12th-century church is Romanesque in style but it underwent restoration in the 18th century. In the transept, there are fine capitals decorated with motifs that are stylised to the point of becoming geometrical patterns. **St. Anne's Chapel,** where the July procession is held, is really in Clohars-Fouesnant 1m. to the north-west of the town. Built near a fountain, it dates from 1685.

The Glénan Archipelago (q.v.) is part of Fouesnant.

Three miles to the south of Fouesnant is **Beg-Meil,** until recently still the "smart" seaside resort. Summer holidays have become less of an upper-class luxury but opulent villas are still hidden from the gaze of the indiscreet amid woods and thickets which dampen the noise of the peak season hustle and bustle.

GLENAN ARCHIPELAGO
Off Fouesnant and Concarneau

The Glénan Archipelago (does its name come from the Celtic word meaning "a small valley"?) is made up of some 10 main islands and several smaller ones. Its marl and sand are used occasionally but today the name of Glénan usually conjures up pictures of the sailing school which was opened on the islands of Penfret, Drenneg, Cigogne and Bananec in 1948.

In summer, the **Ile Saint-Nicolas** is the one that draws the biggest crowds. Boatload upon boatload of holidaymakers come ashore here. The other islands (Geoteg, Kignenek, Cigogne with its old fort, and Le

The Apple Tree Festival in Fouesnant.

Loc'h) attract yachtsmen, scientists from Concarneau's maritime research centre, and ornithologists.

Some of the smaller islands are, in fact, nature reserves. Kastell-Bras provides shelter for shags and herring-gulls ; Kurunenn-Sabl is also the haunt of herring-gulls ; and since 1981 the Ile aux Moutons to the north has been a nesting-place for terns. The heart of the archipelago forms a kind of inland sea called the "Chamber" ; its waters are a very unusual shade of green.

The archipelago was once part of the mainland. A flight over the area indicates quite clearly that the R.Odet once flowed out to here.

The Glénan Islands. ▶
(Photo J.-P. Prével)
An aerial view of the Glénans. ▼
(Photo *Ouest-France*)

GOULVEN
8m. N of Lesneven

This, according to legend, is the land of pagans and wreckers (cf. Plouguerneau). Be that as it may, the sea ebbs over some considerable distance and the strand stretches for miles.

The village has a Gothic **church** (with later restorations). The late 16th-century Renaissance belltower is arguably one of the most charming in the Léon Region.

A road runs along the coast from Goulven to the seaside resort of **Brignogan-Plages** where the shore is dotted with rocks, rather like Ploumanac'h and Trégastel.

GUERLESQUIN
15m. SE of Morlaix

Situated in wild desolate countryside at the point where the Monts d'Arrée meet the Méné Moors, Guerlesquin is a typical Breton village of bygone days. The huge square is surrounded by old granite houses. In the centre, a square building (17th century) with a turret at each corner is the former **courthouse.** The church was rebuilt in 1859.

If you travel south-west to **Lannéanou,** you will find a 'B' road (route départementale) running westwards along the crest of the Monts d'Arrée. **Kerlosser Manor** dates from the 16th century (the fortified redoubt is 15th century).

LE GUILVINEC
6m. SW of Pont-L'Abbé

Life in Le Guilvinec revolves around its fishing port, one of the most colourful in the Bigouden Region.

Kergoz Manor to the north still has its wall and dovecot above the gateway.

St.Fiacre's Chapel (16th century) lies one mile out of Le Guilvinec on the Lesconil road. It has a fountain with a niche built into the wall of the chevet.

Two miles further on lies the port of **Lesconil** where fishing is a small-scale business. Opposite the coastal station is a pile of rocks, the backdrop to a tiny beach.

The harbour at Le Guilvinec.

Guimiliau Church.

Guimiliau : the calvary. ▶

GUIMILIAU
10m. SW of Morlaix

Guimiliau is a quiet little village off the beaten track, but with one of the most remarkable parish closes anywhere in Brittany. It is one of a whole group of 16th- and 17th-century masterpieces that are to be found in the Léon Region.

A **triumphal gateway** leads into the close. On the right stands the great **calvary,** which is very ornate (late 16th century); there are more than 200 statues on it. It retells several episodes from the Life of Jesus (not in any set chronological order) and the statues are dressed in 16th-century costume as was usual at that time.

Like all the closes, this one has an **ossuary,** dating from the mid 17th century. On it is an outside pulpit which was used for open-air sermons, especially on All Souls' Day.

The **South porch** (1606) on the way into the church is typical of the Renaissance style as developed in the Léon Region. The traditional porch is decorated with a whole panoply of

Classical Renaissance designs in kersantite, drawn from architectural treatises by Philibert Delorme, the architect of the Tuileries Palace in Paris, and adapted by local craftsmen.

The **church** is a typical example of Breton Flamboyant Gothic architec-

ture, embellished with a few Renaissance features, but it contains some remarkable late 17th-century furniture corresponding to the spread of the Catholic Counter-Reformation. The baptistry (1675) on the left is a masterpiece of Baroque craftsmanship.

Guimiliau : the triumphal gateway.

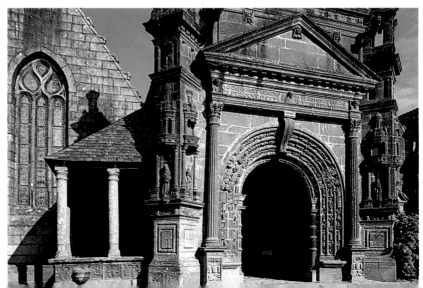

HUELGOAT
19m. S of Morlaix

In Huelgoat (i.e. the Upper Wood), myth is more important than reality. Its forest (dotted with piles of rocks and rushing streams) and its historical and prehistoric remains all give it a very particular meaning for Bretons. In fact, local imagination has peopled all the beauty spots with ghosts, devils, giants, and other supernatural beings.

The village lies on the banks of a lake but new housing estates have taken away some of its charm. On the main square (Place Aristide-Briand where there is a busy open-air market), note the **parish church** (15th and 16th centuries with recent additions), which houses a statue of St. Yves dispensing justice. The **Chapel of Our Lady of Heaven** (Notre-Dame des Cieux) stands in the Rue des Croix; it is a 16th-century building with an 18th-century belltower. It is open to the public (carved painted panels in the chancel).

The usual visit to the natural beauty spots in Huelgoat starts from the lake and more or less follows the course of the R. Argent. The piles of rocks or their strange positions have all been given evocative names like the Mill, the Devil's Cave (which represents the entrance to Hell. A lovely road runs through a deep gorge and down to the banks of the Styx - woe betide anybody who follows it), the Shaking Rock (a huge pile of stone which answers questions by swaying back and forth), the Virgin Mary's household, the Mushroom etc. Visitors with little time to spare usually settle for these sights but they are not the most interesting ones. A few hundred yards into the forest to the north of the Carhaix road, at the end of Lovers' Lane (Sentier des Amoureux), is Artus' Grotto where King Arthur of the Bretons sleeps.

The parish close in **Berrien** 3m. to the north of Huelgoat contains a church (16th century with later alterations) and two calvaries. Nearby is the Kerampeulven Menhir.

Huelgoat.

The Château de Kerjean.(Photo J.-P. Prével)

KERJEAN CASTLE
5m. NW of Landivisiau, in Saint-Vougay

Not far from Le Folgoët and the parish closes, in the heart of the Léon Region, stands **Kerjean Castle,** a Classical Renaissance building (c.1540-1595) that is half-fortress, half-manor. The Saint-Vougay road becomes a majestic beech-lined avenue that is at its most beautiful as the rays of the setting sun filter through the branches. At that moment, the castle's defences stand out at the end of the avenue - walls 40 ft. thick, reinforced at all four corners by casemates, and a curtain wall.

Visitors cross a drawbridge and enter the first courtyard. Then a Renaissance gateway leads into the inner courtyard which is much less austere in appearance. The main building on the left and at the end of the yard has several storeys of windows, the one in the south wing being the most ornate. The main entrance is covered by a portico while in one corner stands a three-pillared well based on a design by the Parisian architect, Jacques Androuët du Cerceau. Similarly elegant is the fountain in the park.

Visitors can stroll though the grounds (Renaissance fountain), tour the castle, or visit the family apartments which are now the Museum of Breton Art and Furniture (16th and 17th centuries).

LAMBADER
11m. W of Morlaix, in Plouvorn

The hamlet of Lambader is particularly attractive for its **chapel** (16th and 17th centuries with later restoration), which stands at the end of a tree-lined avenue. The slender 189-foot belltower was restored in the 19th century.

Inside the church is one of the few wooden rood-screens in Brittany still in its original position. It is Flamboyant Gothic in style. It was built in the late 15th century by a famous workshop in Morlaix. A staircase with traceried arches leads up to an overhanging gallery. The frieze along the balcony depicts the Apostles.

There have been a number of discoveries recently in the **Kernonen Barrow,** which also lies in Plouvorn e.g. daggers decorated with amber beads and gold studs, a bronze dagger, and flint arrowheads.

There are two castles in the area. **Troërin** which was rebuilt in the early 19th century, stands beside a lake in a woodland setting. **Keruzoret,** a mile to the north, is older ; parts of it were built in the second half of the 17th century.

LAMPAUL-GUIMILIAU
16m. SW of Morlaix

The cemetery occupies the centre of the parish close. It has a semi-circular **gateway** topped by three crosses (1668). Beside it is the **ossuary-chapel** (1667).

In the middle of the close stands a very plain calvary (16th century). It comprises three crosses mounted on a single bar at the top of an unfinished column. This is a far cry from Guimiliau with its 200 statues!

The West Front of the church, built in the Gothic style with some Renaissance decoration, is flanked by a belltower (1573) whose spire was struck by a thunderbolt in 1809. The nave and south aisle, in which the window bays are decorated with monsters and other imaginary beasts, both date from the first half of the 16th century and are Flamboyant Gothic in style (except for the piers).

The **south porch** (1533) contains the traditional statues of the twelve Apostles.

There are three real gems of craftsmanship inside the church. First of all, there is the 16th-century **rood-beam** which, of course, bears the Cross and statues of the Virgin Mary and St.John.

The church has a number of reredos but the most richly-decorated are the ones behind the Altar of St.John the Baptist to the right of the chancel and the Passion Altar on the left. The **St.John the Baptist Reredos** depicts, among other things, the life of the saint and certain episodes in the Life of Christ. The bas-reliefs on the side show the fall of the angels. The **Passion Altar Reredos** has eight sections and some of the statues are strikingly realistic. The two side panels are quite ramarkable; one shows the Nativity of the Virgin Mary and the other St.Miliau, King of Cornouaille, who was beheaded but who nevertheless kept his head (as you can see). These altar screens, like so many others, were carved in the late 17th century when Baroque Art was introduced to the region by Jesuit preachers. They add a natural finishing touch to any Breton church. The left-hand aisle contains a **Pietà** with six figures, all of them carved out of a single block of wood. Nearby is the impressive **Burial of Christ** (1676), one of the finest anywhere in Brittany. It was carved by a sculptor from the Navy Establishment in Brest, a man who originally came from the Auvergne.

Lampaul-Guimiliau : the rood beam.

LANDERNEAU
13m. E of Brest

Landerneau, formerly held in fief by the Rohan family, became the capital of the Léon Region in the 16th century. From the 17th to the 19th centuries, the town was a thriving business centre. For many years, a highly-esteemed cloth was produced there and exported to various European countries as well as to French overseas colonies, at least until 1771.

Still, even at the present time, a stroll along the river bank is a pleasant occupation. Pause for a while beside the **Rohan Bridge** (1510) which crosses the R.Elorn. It links two bishoprics - Léon to the north and Cornouaille to the south (they have given their names to the quaysides).

The town is divided into two parishes. To the north lies **St.Houardon's Church** (1860) with a tower and, more especially, a porch (1604) built in the local Renaissance style. The **Church of St.Thomas of Canterbury** to the south dates from the 16th century.

Landerneau : the Rohan Bridge.

Visitors should not leave the town without seeing the streets lined with old houses (17th century), especially near St.Thomas's in the street of the same name and in the Rue des Déportés. Take a look, too, at the fountain on the Place des Quatre-Pompes (1774). On the right bank are the Quai de Léon, the Rue du Commerce, and the market square (on which stands the Rohan Mansion, built in 1662).

The expression "That'll shake them in Landerneau !" comes, according to relevant written sources, from a play by the Breton dramatist Alexandre Duval, "Les Heritiers" (pub. 1796).

Landévennec : the ruins of the former abbey.

LANDEVENNEC
32m. N of Quimper

Surrounded by greenery and trees (beech, pines, chestnut and even palms), lying within a meander of the gentle R.Aulne before it flows out into the sea at Brest, the Landévennec Peninsula attracts visitors because of its mild climate and beautiful scenery.

This is the country of Gwénolé, or Winwaloe. He was born in Armorica, the son of Fragan and Gwen who had emigrated from the British Isles in the 5th century. As befits a future saint, his youth was marked by piety and wisdom. While still a novice, Winwaloe performed a number of miracles. He put back his sister's eye after it had been pecked out and eaten by an angry goose. Winwaloe caught hold of the culprit, opened its stomach, retrieved the eye and put it back in the empty socket.

In the meantime, the saint had become friendly with "King" Gradlon who was not particularly known for his virtue. Under Winwaloe's influence, he was converted to Christianity and he withdrew to the town of Ys which was then a den of vice and fornication. Divine punishment was at hand (cf. Douarnenez) but Winwaloe managed to save Gradlon in the nick of time.

In 913 A.D. the monastery was destroyed by the Vikings. It was rebuilt and became one of Brittany's foremost spiritual and intellectual centres. For centuries, its sphere of influence was considerable but the French Revolution put a stop to all that. Thanks to the enthusiasm of Father Perrot, renewed interest began to be shown in the abbey by 1935. In 1950, the Benedictines of Kerbénéat purchased Landévennec and decided to rebuild the monastery.

All that remains of the old **abbey** (on the site or in the museum) are a few pre-Romanesque features but most of the building dates from the 11th century. There is one old statue of St.Winwaloe (possibly 12th century?). The south transept houses a tomb said to be that of King Gradlon.

Landévennec : a statue of St.Winwaloe.

Near the shore is the present-day church ; its spire dates back to the 17th century.

To the south between the meander at Térénez and the Landévennec Peninsula, is **Le Folgoat Wood** where there is a lake, an old seapowered mill, and a chapel. Five miles to the south-east lies the **Térénez Bridge,** which was destroyed in 1944 and brought back into service in 1957. The bridge stands some 97 ft. above the R.Aulne and is 885 ft. long. The coast road from Térénez to Le Faou is particularly attractive.

LANDIVISIAU
14m. W of Morlaix

Landivisiau, in the heart of the Léon Region, is often mentioned in connection with its fairs and markets. But anybody interested in architecture will doubtless prefer its **parish church,** which was originally dedicated to St.Thuriaff, or Thivisiau, Bishop of Dol in the 8th century. The present building is modern but it has integrated a few features from its predecessor e.g. the Flamboyant Gothic and early Renaissance

The Aulne Valley.

side porch (1554) and its arching decorated with scenes from the Old Testament.

LANMEUR
8m. NE of Morlaix

The village lies on the site of the former Kerfeunten, or town of the fountain, which was razed to the ground by the Vikings in the 9th century. There are still some traces of the old town left e.g. a Romanesque or pre-Romanesque **crypt** below the present church, which is modern apart from the 18th-century tower.

The crypt is the only one of its kind in Brittany.

The **Chapel of Our Lady of Kernitron** was built by the Knights Templars in the 12th century and extended in the 16th century.

To the north beyond **Guimaëc** stands Kergadiou Manor. In the same village, but to the north-west, is the 16th-century Christ's Chapel. The road leads to the **Pointe de Beg-an-Fri** (i.e. the tip of the nose).

The Chapel of Our Lady of Joy (16th - 17th centuries) contains a late 16th-century chancel.

LAZ
5m. S of Châteauneuf-du-Faou

Deposited in the cemetery at the west end of the village is the **calvary** dating from 1527. The Virgin Mary is dressed in a mourning cloak. The **church** dates from the 18th century; its Purgatory Reredos is an incitement to good behaviour.

In modern Breton, "lazh" meaning "murder". According to legend, Daoulas (two murders?) gets its name from a double killing but this etymology is doubtful. A less romantic, if more likely meaning is

"a river" (from the adjective "glas" taken as a noun).

From the end of the village on the Châteauneuf road, the view stretches over the foothills of the Montagnes Noires (**Signal de Laz,** alt.990 ft.).

To the east towards Roudouallec, the road passes the **Castell-Ruffel Belvedere** (alt.943 ft.) where there is a passage grave.

The 15th-century **Pontouar Chapel** lies three miles to the south-west in Trégourez.

LESNEVEN
16m. NE of Brest

Lesneven has long been an urban centre and its rich history is presented in the Léon Museum, opened in 1986. **St.Michael's Church** (1755-1763) is of little importance except for the Renaissance porch which belonged to an earlier building. There are some 17th-century **houses** on the main square.

LOCQUIREC
14m. NE of Morlaix

Locquirec lies in a particularly beautiful setting on a peninsula, opposite Locquémeau. The road from Plestin crosses the Douron, the small river marking the boundary between Finistère and Côtes-du-Nord, by a bridge 338 yds. long.

The Knights Templars had a community in Locquirec. The church, with its 17th-century tower, stands in the middle of the former cemetery which still has some of its old gravestones. Inside the church, 17th- and 18th-century paintings adorn the arches in the transept and chancel. The carvings on the reredos behind the High Altar depict scenes from Christ's Passion.

◀ *Locronan : general view* (photo by Maurice Dilasser).   *The town square in Locronan.*

LOCRONAN

10m. NW of Quimper

This small village with a population of only 700 probably constitutes the finest example of vernacular architecture in Lower Brittany.

In the centre of the evenly-paved **square** stands a well. Round about is a unique group of stone-built houses dating from the 16th and 17th centuries when the canvas industry ensured the town's prosperity. Locronan supplied sailcloth to the Spanish navy, the port of Brest, and the French East India Company. The industry fell into decline just before the French Revolution. Today, hand-weaving has begun again and Locronan has become a craft centre. The village has a small museum which is open during the tourist season.

Standing side by side are the intercommunicating **St.Ronan's Church** (15th century) and the 15th- and 16th-century **Pénity Chapel.** The church tower is a replica of the ones

in Quimper, built in the Anglo-Norman style; the spire collapsed in 1808. The slightly-projecting north porch has a festooned door while, in front of the tower on the West Front, another porch has ogival arches. The cemetery contains a calvary on which St.Ronan and the Virgin Mary stand on either side of the crucified Christ. It is from the end of the cemetery that the beauty of the building is most obvious, with the great flat chevet containing the main window that is typical of Breton Gothic architecture.

The church is built in an overall uniform style. Building began in 1420 and was completed in 1480 with the inclusion of the main window. Inside, there is a stone-vaulted roof, a rarity in Brittany. Carved on the pillars and great arches are slender ribs uninterrupted by capitals, in the Flamboyant Gothic style that was adopted in the magnificent buildings designed in Brittany in the 15th and 16th centuries. Because of the lie of

the land, the church is built on two levels. The ten medallions round the pulpit tell the story of St. Ronan; they were carved by one Louis Bariou. In the right-hand side aisle, there is a striking example of late mediaeval wood carving in the statue of Christ awaiting his torturers. Other statues represent St. Ronan, St. Corentin, and St. Christopher. The **Rosary Reredos** dates from 1668. The sacristy houses the church's treasure.

Eaten away by a green slime caused by the underground springs below the building, the Pénity Chapel houses a large stone polychrome statue of **The Lamentation of Mary** (1517) and **St. Ronan's Tomb** on which the saint is seen dressed in his vestments and wearing a mitre. The kersantite monument dates from the mid 15th century.

At the end of a steeply-sloping alley that runs uphill from the north end of the square stands the **Chapel of Our Lady of Good News** (Notre-

Dame de Bonne Nouvelle, 15th to 17th centuries), which has a small Renaissance lantern turret. Inside, there is a 16th-century carving of Christ being laid in the tomb. The fountain dates from 1698.

Every six years (1983, 1989, 1995 etc.), an almost unique procession is held in Locronan, the **Grand Troménie**, probably a deformation of "tro minic'hi" or "tour of the monastery lands". It covers 7 1/2 to 8 miles and people process through the countryside along the route supposedly taken by the saint every week. The ceremony begins on a Sunday morning in July with the saluting of the banners. In the afternoon, the solemn procession gets underway to the sound of drums. There are stops before each of the 44 resting-places along the route - small shelters made of branches covered with white sheets beneath which are statues from Locronan itself and from neighbouring parishes. Each shelter is the responsibility of a church-warden whose bell indicates his presence. The faithful process up the moutainside to St.Ronan's Chapel (modern) and round a block of granite known as "Kador Sant Ronan" (St. Ronan's Chair) which locals insist is the boat on which Ronan came to Armorica from Ireland. In days gone by, women with sterility problems used to come and sit in it. As for the **Minor Troménie**, it is held every year, on the second Sunday in July, unless there is to be a Grand Troménie. The route covers 2 1/2 to 3 miles.

Möellien Manor (17th century) lies a mile to the NW of Locronan.

LOCTUDY
16m. SW of Quimper

This seaside resort has the best-preserved **Romanesque church** in Brittany. Visitors should not be put off by the outside of the church and its tower, both of which date from 1760. The barrel-vaulted chancel, the groined arches in the ambulatory and the apsidal chapels are all splendid pieces of architecture. The nave, lit by a clerestory, has cruciform pillars. The capitals are decorated not only with crossettes, palmettes and spirals but also with crosses, animals, and human figures. They are a reinterpretation in granite of traditional Corinthian capitals. On several of the bases are quite distinct carvings of naked men and women. Although not as explicit as certain Indian carvings, one of the bas-reliefs is fairly licentious.

Top right : *Locronan : the Troménie procession* (photo by René Coroller).

Locronan : the filming of "Les Chouans", directed by Philippe de Broca.   Bottom right : *The harbour at Loctudy.*

The style of the early 12th-century building, which underwent restoration between 1845 and 1888, was influenced by its mother church, the Benedictine abbey in Saint-Gildas-de-Rhuys, and consequently by the architecture of the Loire Valley.

From the **harbour,** there is a view across the quietly-flowing pine tree-lined river of Pont-L'Abbé which widens into an estuary dotted with islands before finally reaching the sea. One of the roads to Pont-L'Abbé follows the wooded riverside. Across the strait, **Ile Tudy** is a narrow strip of land on which huddle fishermen's cottages and a winding network of alleyways. Outside the village, on the Pont-L'Abbé road, an Irish or Celtic cross stands next to the **Croaziou Chapel** (partly 14th century).

Half-a-mile further on, **Kérazan Castle** (late 16th century but with 18th-century alterations) houses an art gallery with paintings and drawings by Jean de Mabuse, Maurice Denis, Théodore Gudin, Désiré Lucas etc.

LOCUNOLE
8m. NE of Quimperlé

The rushing waters of the R.Ellé are dominated by an impressive mass of gigantic stones - the **Devil's Rocks.** Tradition has it that St. Winwaloe, charmed by the strangeness of the setting, built his hermitage here. Satan, who was master of the place, wanted to chase him out but was defeated by a ruse. Winwaloe may have been a saint but he was crafty with it.

LOPEREC
8m. SE of Le Faou

St.Pérec's Church underwent major restoration and alterations between 1860 and 1894. The tower dates from almost the same period as the façade, which has an interesting doorway (1666) decorated with Corinthian columns and a pediment below the niche containing the statue of St.Pérec.

The porch dates from 1586. Inside, are statues of the Apostles (1615) and corbels. The chancel and sacristy are very late 17th century. In the church, note the font and the reredos. The calvary (1557), which had recently been restored, was very badly damaged by the October 1987 hurricane.

Further west in the cemetery in **Quimerc'h,** there is a cross with a number of figures on it (late 16th century). The porch (1621) comes from Old Quimerc'h.

Pont-de-Buis-les-Quimerc'h is especially well-known for its powder magazine which was established in 1688. In June 1795, a group of some 600 Royalist rebels took it by storm.

LA MARTYRE
6m. E of Landerneau

This is one of the most subtle yet richest parish closes in the whole of Brittany. It bears witness to the amazing prosperity of a parish that was once one of Europe's major trading posts. People travelled from Ireland and Flanders to attend its fairs.

At the entrance to the close, above the **triumphal arch** (15th century) is

Meilars : Notre-Dame de Confort.

La Martyre : the parish close.

a platform and a 16th-century calvary. Carvings on the very fragile porch (c.1450) illustrate the life of Christ and give some insight into contemporary society. There is also a realistic sculpture of the benefactor, the abbot of Daoulas. On the tympanum is a later carving representing the Virgin Mary in bed. The shafts and arches of the porch are covered with cherubs and human figures. The porch also contains a stoup with Ankou, or Death, on it (1601). The ossuary dates from 1619. It was built by the Kerjean workshop, using fine kersantite.

On the outside wall is a sheathed **caryatid** taken straight out of the French Renaissance books on architecture. On the monumental pediment is a statue of St.Pol-Aurélien, patron saint of Saint-Pol-de-Léon.

The most striking feature inside the church is the total lack of stylistic cohesion.

MEILARS
3m. E of Pont-Croix

Standing on the roadside, the **church of Notre-Dame de Confort** (i.e. Our Lady of Comfort or Succour) was built c.1528-1550. The double-galleried tower 104 ft. high dates from 1736. The West Front is decorated with 13 statues dating from the 16th century. In the centre is a statue of St.Michael the Archangel. Note also the carved caravels. On the south wall, there are caryatids (perhaps representing the deadly sins ?).

Inside, there are 16th- and 17th-century **corbels.** Some of the carvings were considered to be too licentious and were either destroyed or altered. The stained glass windows date from the mid 16th century, e.g. the main window with its Rod of Jesse. But Confort is especially famous for its **carillon drum** (12 bells) which was rung above the heads of children who were totally dumb or who were afflicted with some speech defect. There are six other such drums in Brittany, and a few others in the Pyrenees, Spain, Portugal, and Italy. According to Gwenc'hlan Le Scouëzec, Egyptian priests used to rotate similar drums in the temples of the sun gods. The drum or wheel is the symbol of continual change and perpetual return.

The main part of the **calvary** (note the subtlety of the decoration) dates from the second half of the 16th century but the statues of the Apostles were added in 1870 (the original sculptures were destroyed during the French Revolution).

In Poullan-sur-Mer a mile to the north-east, the **Chapel of Our Lady of Kérinec** is one of the finest examples of the Pont-Croix school (semicircular arcades c.1280).

MENEZ-HOM

9m. W of Châteaulin, in Dinéault

Lying at the westernmost end of the Montagnes Noires, Menez-Hom (or Menez-C'hom) with its slopes covered in megalithic monuments, looks down on the whole of Western Brittany from its 1,072 ft. The view is quite outstanding. In very fine weather, it stretches as far as the Baie de Douarnenez, the Montagnes Noires, the Arcoat, the Rade de Brest, the Aulne Estuary, and the Crozon Peninsula. According to certain legends, King Marc'h is buried nearby beside the Trégarven road. Because of his sins, he is at present persona non grata in Heaven. He will not be allowed in until he can see the tower of the Chapel of St.Mary of Menez-Hom from his saddle. He is in for a long wait, but erosion is doing what it can to help him.

The name Menez-Hom has, of course, excited lively interet among etymologists. Some people have spoken of the Druids' cauldron, but the word "komm" which now means a "trough" originally meant a "valley" (it is said to be the equivalent of the Old French "combe", a word of Celtic origin). The summit of Menez-Hom lies within the boundary of **Dinéault.** The famous statue of "Bridget", now in the Breton Museum in Rennes, was discovered in Kerguilly in Dinéault in 1913. It dates from the first half of the 1st century.

The **Chapel of St.Mary of Menez-Hom,** 2m. to the south in Plomodiern, is a real oasis in this landscape of bare moorland and isolated pine trees. Beyond the semi-circular arched gateway (1739) is the close containing a calvary dating from 1544.

The Gothic and Renaissance church was built mainly in the period 1570-1591. The 17th-century belltower, with two galleries and a lantern turret, is a modest replica of the ones in Saint-Thégonnec and Lampaul-Ploudalmézeau. Inside the church, the three early 18th-century **reredos** are impressive for their exuberance.

The Menez-Hom.

The harbour at Doëlan.

MOELAN
6m. SW of Quimperlé

The **Chapel of St.Philibert and St.Roch** (16th century) to the south of the village has a typical Cornouaillais belltower based on the one on St.Fiacre's Chapel in Le Faouët. Worthy of note are the small 16th-century calvary and, inside the church, a 17th-century reredos. The parish **church** has five Baroque confessionals (18th century) like the ones found in Bavaria; they were installed here by Jesuit missionaires. Near the village, on the Riec road, is the **Kergoustance** passage grave (Late Stone Age). The village has a large number of Stone Age monuments.

The coastline near Moëlan, between Kerfany and Le Pouldu, is indented with rias. Tiny fishing and yachting harbours like Doëlan, Brigneau, and Merrien nestle on the shore in the midst of pine woods. **Kerfany-les-Pins** lies at the mouth of the R.Bélon. It is a cluster of bungalows hidden among the pines that overlook the sea. The R.Bélon itself is prettier. It is famous for its oyster beds which are accessible either from Lorient on the left bank or from the small port of Bélon on the right bank.

Within the boundaries of **Riec-sur-Bélon,** 3m. to the west of the village, lies the harbour of Rosbras. From here, there are some quite remarkable views of the gentle landscape formed by the wooded banks of the R.Aven.

LES MONTAGNES NOIRES

This is perhaps the true Brittany; it is the most secretive in any case. Yet it is less popular with the tourists who, instead of discovering things for themselves, prefer to follow sign-posted and busy paths and roads. The Montagnes Noires (Menezioù Du, in Breton) are, in fact, rolling hills. The highest point is **Roc'h Toul-Laeron** (i.e. the thieves' cave, alt. 1,060 ft.) in Spézet to the north of Gourin. The "Black Mountains" are, therefore, much lower than the Monts d'Arrée (1,248 ft. at Tuchenn-ar-Gador).

Like them, though, the Montagnes Noires consist of hard sandstone and quartzite. The extensive forests which once covered their slopes (hence their name perhaps) have now disappeared; only the Laz Forest and a few minor woodlands remain.

Although divided between three counties, the Montagnes Noires are really all part of Cornouaille, for the Diocese of Quimper once spread its tentacles far out to the north-east.

MORLAIX

36m. E of Brest

There are numerous traces of the old town (once the third largest in Brittany) but the appearance of the 16th- and 17th-century city has altered considerably. The **viaduct** above the town, which seems to crush the houses below, dates from 1863. It is 191 ft. high and 958 ft. long. It was required for the Paris-Brest railway line, but its construction led to the disappearnace of old houses with lancet windows on the banks of the R.Le Dossen.

To visit the town, leave from the Place des Otages in the centre. To the north is the viaduct; to the south the town hall (1845). Near the viaduct on the east side of the square is a flight of stone steps leading to **St.Melaine's Church.** It is built in the Flamboyant Gothic style and has a modern lantern tower, a fine 17th-century organ, old furnishings, and a rare statue of St. Rose of Lima, the patron saint of the New World.

To the left of the steps, note the Hôtel du Parc (Breton Renaissance). Take the Rue **Ange-de-Guernisac**

behind the church; it is lined with corbelled houses built of local stone (granite and blue schist). From the Place de Viarmes, head for the Place des Jacobins, not by way of the very busy Rue d'Aiguillon but via the picturesque Rue du Fil. If you are a good walker, you can climb the steps in the Venelle des Fontaines and follow the Rue Sainte-Marthe up to Carmel. The Carmelite fountain backs onto the former front of the chapel. On the Place des Jacobins is the former Dominican church, now a **museum** after having been used as

Morlaix: general view.

a barracks. Inside, the view is broken up by a mezzanine. However, the 15th-century rose window at the end of the former chancel is still there for all to see and admire. The States of Brittany met here three times.

How about a stroll beyond the Dominican convent, along the picturesque Allée du Poan-Ben where the R.Jarlot flows in the open air. When you get to the Paris road, turn right into the Rue des Bouchers and go on to **St.Matthew's Church.** All that remains of the old building is the large 16th-century tower.

From the church, go down the Rue du Mur to the Place des Halles which is lined with **old houses** (including Queen Anne's House). Most of them have "lanterns", i.e. the spiral staircase inside is lit by a bay window or lantern.

◀ *Old Morlaix.*

Rue Ange-de-Guernisac in Morlaix. ▶

Morlaix : marina and tobacco factory. ▼

ILE D'OUESSANT (USHANT)
Off l'Aber-Ildut and Le Conquet.

Everybody knows the Breton proverb that runs, "He who sees Belle-Ile sees an island ; he who sees Groix sees joy ; he who sees Ushant sees blood". It is an allusion to the dangers of navigation in the sea of Ushant, dotted with reefs and pounded by storms. The islanders themselves seldom venture out in small boats, for they consider it to be too dangerous even though fish is particularly abundant in these waters. Moreover, sea mist is a frequent hazard, and the currents (especially Fromrust and Fromveur) race here.

When winter comes, the wind takes over the island, shaking it continuously for weeks on end, flattening out a landscape that is no longer used for farming (although the locals do grow potatoes). The few trees huddle on valley floors. A storm on Ushant really is an event that takes on sinister importance what with the whistling of the wind, the sheets of rain that lash the shore, and the wailing of sirens. Not to mention the beam from one of the most powerful lighthouses in the world as it pierces the darkness to warn ships of approaching danger.

Yet in springtime the cries of migrating birds remind the islanders that summer is not far away and that fine weather is just around the corner. In summer, the weather is often very good and, even if the landlubbers sometimes find the crossing a bit choppy, it is not dangerous at this time of year. The island is an exceptionally good place for bird watching ; 250 species have been spotted here.

Four miles long and two-and-a-half miles wide, Ushant (Ouessant in French, and Enez-Eussa in Breton from the Gallic "Uxisana" meaning "the highest") is a totally different world. The houses are usually single-storey buildings with five windows and one door (wisely turning its back on the wind). There is some new housing, probably too much of it in fact, hence the official decision to include Ushant in the Armorica Regional Park. Here and there are white or black sheep, short-legged animals as if to be better protected from the wind.

On Ushant, it was traditionally the women who asked the men to marry them. Much to the regret of the shy members of the population, this custom has now died out. Its origins are easy to explain - there are not many men on Ushant. They all join the

◀ *The island of Callot and the Baie de Morlaix.*

Ushant : the folk museum.

Two views of the north coast of Ushant. ▶
▶

Navy or board merchant vessels and sail to the four corners of the globe. The women, then, lead a particularly lonely life. Their traditional costume reflected their lifestyle - it was as black as a storm. In days gone by, when an Ushant man was lost at sea, the islanders would pray until dawn in his house, then carry a small Cross called a "broela" or "proela" (said by some to mean "the return home") in a funeral casket from the church. Later, the casket was taken into the mausoleum in the graveyard.

You should go as the mood takes you on the island but be sure not to miss the extraordinary **north-west coast** between the Baie de Béninou and the **Créac'h Lighthouse,** Ushant's main tourist attraction (Créac'h comes from "Krec'h" meaning "a hill"). The lighthouse, just over a mile from the village of Lampaul, was opened in 1862 but was not to become one of the most powerful in the world until 1939. With its 500 million candlepower, it has a range of 124 miles.

The **Pointe du Pern** not far away (two miles from the village) has rocks shaped like animals. The island itself is shaped like a crab's pincer. **Nividic Lighthouse** is uninhabited because it is controlled directly from Ushant. It can only be reached by helicopter.

To the north-east is the **Pointe du Stiff** (from which there is also an interesting view). And we must mention the **Pointe de Pen-al-Lann** to the east and the **Pointe de Pen-ar-Roc'h** to the south-east. If you are lucky, you may even spot a colony of grey seals during one of your walks round the island.

The main village is **Lampaul.** It was named after St. Pol Aurélien who landed on the island to convert the inhabitants to Christianity (cf.Batz). The village has a number of old houses and, in the cemetery, the monument (1688) containing the broelaoù (Crosses) of those lost at sea. In Nion-Huella, a mile from the village are the two **Centres of Ushant Techniques and Traditions.**

Molène, the usual stopover between Ushant and the mainland, is much smaller. It is a flat island not quite a mile long and slightly more than half-a-mile wide. It is said that a cow never has all four hooves in the same field because the plots of land are so minute. Unlike their neighbours on Ushant, the islanders earn their living from fishing (especially shellfish), selling their catches in Le Conquet. There is also some farming and, from April to September, the inhabitants gather seaweed, a highly-reputed fertiliser (nicknamed "Molène ash"). Although it is less given to tourism than Ushant, Molène will enchant those who appreciate solitude.

Houses on Ushant.

PENMARC'H
19m. SW of Quimper

This is a linguist's dream. Penmarc'h is a translation of the old name, Cap Caval (which itself comes from the Latin "Caput Caballi"). The name, then, means "horse's head".

In the 16th century, Penmarc'h was a densely-populated prosperous town specialising in cod-fishing. It was, in fact, one of Europe's foremost ports. In 1595, the Leaguer-brigand Guy Eder de la Fontenelle rampaged through the neighbourhood, ransomed the population, slaughtered some of the inhabitants, and had the ships taken to his hideout on the Ile Tristan off Tréboul (Douarnenez).

The gateway into the parish close is a 16th-century basket-handle arch. **St.Nonna's Church** is dedicated to a holy man who came from Ireland c. 6th century. Building began in 1508

Penmarc'h : the Eckmühl Lighthouse. ▶

Fortified chapel and coastal station at Penmarc'h. ▼

in the Flamboyant Gothic style, and the size of the church is proof of the community's erstwhile prosperity. The openwork tower is reminiscent of the one in Tronoën. Note the semi-circular arches in the porch (also 1508). The walls of the tower, which has never been completed, are decorated with fish, smacks and caravels. The church has a large number of 16th- and 17th-century statues.

Magdalen Chapel (15th century) has six stained glass windows (1981) by the painter Jean Bazaine (b. 1904, Paris). The chapel once stood in the lepers' graveyard (hence its name; Mary Magdalen was the patron saint of lepers).

Kérity in the south-west is a fishing harbour. St. Thunette's Church (early 16th century) was restored in 1950.

From the top of the **Eckmühl Lighthouse** (208 ft. high, 307 steps up to the lamp), the view extends across the Penmarc'h Plain with its raggle-taggle housing development. The lighthouse, opened in 1897, was built thanks to a legacy from Madame de Blocqueville, the daughter of Maréchal Davout, Prince of Eckmühl (which explains how a Breton lighthouse comes to have the same name as a Bavarian village). Beneath it, the tiny port of Saint-Pierre nestles against the old lighthouse, St. Peter's Chapel (15th century) and a coastal station.

Further along the road to Saint-Guénolé is the **Chapel of Our Lady of Joy** (15th century).

After a look out to sea beyond the rocks at Saint-Guénolé, it would be appropriate to stop for a while at the **Finistère Museum of Prehistory** (which is run by Rennes University). The exhibits are the result of all the modern digs carried out in the county.

Beyond the beach at Pors-Carn, on the Pointe de la Torche, are the ruins of a **passage grave** with side chambers. A number of prehistoric remains have been uncovered on the headland.

PLABENNEC
9m. N of Brest

St. Tenenan's Church dates from 1720 but the south porch and tower were built one century earlier. The close has two ossuaries.

Plouvien, to the north-west, has several manor houses (including Kerbreder, 15th century) and two interesting churches - the 15th-century St.John's (note the Baptism of Christ on the tympanum) and the more interesting **St. Jaoua's** (early 16th century) which some people consider to be one of the most charming churches in the Léon Region. Note the arcaded ossuary and the 17th-century fountain. Jaoua was the nephew of St.Pol-Aurélien.

◀ *Penmarc'h : the Saint-Guénolé rocks.*

Traditional headdresses can still be seen in Penmarc'h. ▶

Pointe de la Torche (photo by Noël Guiriec).

The calvary at Pleyben.

PLEYBEN
21m. N of Quimper

The parish close in Pleyben is a quite exceptional architectural gem. Take the **monumental gateway** (1725) into the old graveyard ; above it are a Pietà and a statue of the Crucifixion. From there, you can see the **ossuary,** or funeral chapel (1550) which is one of the oldest in Brittany. Its architecture is carefully-designed, as is shown by the surbased arches that decorate the openings in the façade.

The **church** (1564 but with late 19th-century restoration) has two towers. One of them, topped by an elegantly powerful Gothic spire, is connected to a bell-turreted staircase tower by a footbridge. The other tower is a less airy, more dignified construction ; it seems to be solidly fixed to the ground from which it rises. This Renaissance **belltower,** adapted from the great Anglo-

Pleyben : the parish close.

Norman towers to suit the new architectural style (it was begun in 1588 and completed in 1642) has a dome with lantern turrets. It was used as a prototype for a number of towers throughout Brittany. On the south side is the niche of St. Germain, Bishop of Auxerre, the patron saint of the parish and the highly-esteemed master of several local Breton saints. On sentry duty in the porch are the Apostles, ready to welcome visitors. The **sacristy** (1719), which was built to a Bramante-style design, is dominated by a lanterned cupola and barrel vaulting.

Inside the church, experts will appreciate the quality of workmanship in the timbered roof (16th century). On the carved corbels (1571), there is a plethora of designs, a kaleidoscope of motifs that are both naïve and realistic - a piper, skulls, and devils.

Although the church is interesting, it is the **calvary** that is the real masterpiece in Pleyben. For many years, it was believed to date from the 17th century because the date 1650 was carved on it. Yet in this case, it was difficult to explain why the statues were all dressed in the 16th-century costume (unless the sculptor simply wanted to imitate his predecessors). Today, however, it seems to be generally accepted that 1650 was the year in which the monument underwent restoration and that it was originally erected c.1555.

PLOMELIN
6m. S of Quimper

The R.Odet is a joy to behold as its flows from Quimper to the sea. Its wooded banks and winding course lead boat-trippers into a charming secret landscape. On the right bank to the north-east of Plomelin, there are two manorhouses, near the Baie de Kerogan - **Kerdour** (16th century with later alterations) and **Keraval** (15-16th centuries) which has one of only four Breton anguipedes.

The area is not always easy to reach. You will need detailed maps, maybe even a compass, and you will have to ask your way as you go. Yet some of the routes are signposted from Quimper. Taking the **Castle Route** (Route des Châteaux) to Pont-L'Abbé, you will come to the Gorre-Bodivit road junction just beside a wayside Cross. It tails off into a path that runs steeply down to the shore. Nearby are the ruins of a **Roman villa,** the Villa Flamius. Half-a-mile further on, the Kerouzien lane leads to a **vantage point** from which there is an outstanding view of the R.Odet. The **Château de Pérennou** (late 19th century) has superb English-style gardens. Still on the Pont-L'Abbé road, at St. Roch's Chapel, take the Penvellet path which passes the **Lestrémeur Manor** (once the property of Madame de Sévigné) and leads to the shore near the spot where the R. Odet flows into the Combrit cove.

Les Vire-Court, a beauty spot to the east of Plomelin, is the best-known point of access to the R.Odet. The river flows from one meander to the next between steeply-sloping banks. A rock known as the **Maiden's Leap** is a reminder of the wonderfully good man who helped across the river a young girl who feared for her virtue. Times have changed.

Gouesnac'h on the left bank still has its high-banked lanes and vegetable plots. **St. Cadou's Chapel** (16th century) is the meeting-place of wrestlers in the summer. **Lanuron** to the south-west is an 18th-century country residence.

The Odet Valley.

PLONEOUR-LANVERN
4m. NW of Pont-L'Abbé

The **Chapel of Our Lady of Languivoa** to the east of the village lies in ruins but has been saved from total destruction by a group of young people who were the prizewinners of the "Masterpieces in Danger" competition. The chancel, based on the one in Languidou (cf.Plovan), dates from the 13th century but the building was damaged during the War of Breton Succession (1340-1365). In 1386, a papal bull granted indulgences to anybody who volunteered to help with its restoration. The tower, which was decapitated in 1675 after the Red Bonnet Revolt, was built in 1638.

PLOUARZEL
14m. NW of Brest

Some two miles to the east of the village on the Saint-Renan road is the **Kerloas Menhir** which, at 33 ft., is the tallest standing stone in Brittany. Kerloas lies 400 ft. above sea level. Not far away is the 17th-century **Kervéatoux Manor.**

From **Trézien** to the west of Plouarzel, a road runs down to the **Pointe de Corsen** (Alt. 101 ft.). From the clifftop, there is a view across the Chenal du Four to the islands of Molène and Ushant. The headland, though seldom visited, is actually the most westerly point of mainland France. A short distance to the north is the **Trézien lighthouse.** The view from the top (180 steps) is even more breathtaking.

PLOUESCAT
9m. W of Saint-Pol-de-Léon

Plouescat, a centre of fishing and market gardening, has a **covered market** with rafters dating from the 16th century. But the town is better-known for all that it has to offer in the way of excursions. The **Kernic passage grave** stands on the beach to the west. It is one of the many Stone Age monuments in the town.

▲ *Chapel of Notre-Dame de Languivoa.*

◄ *The passage grave in Kernic*
(photo by N. Fediaevsky).

Plouézoc'h : the Barnénez barrow.

PLOUEZOC'H
6m. N of Morlaix

Plouezoc'h has a 17th-century church but it is the **Barnenez Barrow** which attracts the most attention. It is one of the largest prehistoric monuments in Brittany, standing on a promontory overlooking the mouth of the Morlaix river.

Built in the Stone Age, it is a double cairn with eleven passage graves. The eastern end comprises five large tombs, narrow corridors 23-26ft. in length. At the end of one of these corridors are two chambers. Note the symbols carved on the walls ; there are even three axes and a bow on one of the pillars. The western section has six dolmens. In one of them, the so-called ''A'' Dolmen, are several inscriptions in the shape of a capital ''U''. Nine of the chambers in the cairn are roofed with false domes. The eastern section is said to date from 4,600-4,300 B.C. It is an impressive building feat (224 ft. long, 20-26 ft. high, 65-81 ft. wide) and one of the largest cairns in Europe.

An aerial view of the Barnénez barrow.

PLOUGASNOU
9m. NE of Morlaix

St. Peter's Church is mainly 16th century but some parts of it are much older. On the south front, note the Renaissance porch and the seignorial chapel. The tower (1583) has balustraded galleries on the south side. Inside, the most interesting features are the 16th-century font and the large Rosary reredos (1668). The parish also has a funeral chapel (1580) and an open-air pulpit, both of them now in the cemetery on the La Grève road.

Le Cosquer Manor, which stands near the shore, was built in the 15th century but has undergone extensive alterations this century.

Plougastel : A close-up of the Calvary.
An open-air Mass near Plougastel.

The calvary in Plougastel-Daoulas.

PLOUGASTEL-DAOULAS
6m. E of Brest

In Plougastel, only the magnificent **calvary** (1604) has survived. It was damaged during the air raids of 1944 but has been skilfully restored. There are 150 figures on it.

"The style of the Plougastel calvary," wrote Eugène Royer, "provides a sense of interiority, a sort of gravity and slowness of move-ment.." And Yves-P. Castel adds, "Plougastel is a return to order, with a certain rigour, a grain of mineral impassibility, unless one prefers to see in it the all-enveloping serenity of holiness." The figures only come to life in the south-west corner where you can see the dragon with its mouth open ready to gobble up Katell Gollet, Catherine the Damned, the woman of easy virtue whose story is the subject of a popular song.

A mile to the east is the **White Fountain Chapel** (15th-16th centuries). Fragments of a **fertility (or virility) statue** were discovered nearby in 1975.

The Plougastel-Daoulas **peninsula,** the stronghold of strawberry-growers and early vegetable producers, has a plethora of tiny chapels.

L'Aber Wrac'h.

PLOUGONVEN
7m. SE of Morlaix

The Flamboyant Gothic **church** (1481-1532, with later restoration) has a balconied belltower with a staircase tower. The **ossuary** dates from 1532; trefoiled arcading decorates the windows. The **chapel** with its lantern-turrets, however, is less impressive; it was built in 1746.

The **calvary** was erected in 1554 but underwent major, if not always skilful, restoration in 1898.

PLOUGUERNEAU
18m. N of Brest

Plouguerneau lies at the heart of wild country - a ragged coastline, bare sand dunes, and a flat windy hinterland. The Guissény region to the east is "pagan country", or Bro-Bagan in Breton (from the Latin "paganus" meaning "pagan" and "peasant"). To the west beyond the dunes are the abers, deep estuaries that cut into the shore. The Breton word "aber" means "mouth of a river".

Plouguerneau is said to have been built on the site of a city that has long since disappeared, called Tolente. Its name is mentioned in several ancient texts. It has gained a reputation of being a huge mysterious town, the capital of Armorica. And why not indeed? It is said to have been destroyed by the Vikings in the 9th century.

Just over two miles to the south-east stands the church of **Our Lady of Grouannec** (14th and early 16th centuries, restored in 1954), a country chapel with stained glass windows by Max Ingrand.

As you go in search of Tolente, you may like to travel along the coast north of Plouguerneau, where the most interesting beauty spots are as follows:

— the **Virgin Mary Lighthouse** (1902) on the island that also bears Her name. At 250 ft., this is one of the tallest lighthouses in France. On terra firma, the resort of Lilia has a certain charm.

— **Saint-Michel** is Plouguerneau's yachting harbour. In a pleasant setting stands St. Michael's Chapel, and a shrine at which a local man, Dom Mikaël Le Nobletz, came to pray. He it was who converted the neighbourhood to Christianity in the 17th century.

Back in Plouguerneau, cross the bridge that spans the Aber Wrac'h at Paluden. The road takes you to **Lannilis,** a charming little village and an excellent place from which to explore the strip of land that lies between the **Aber Wrac'h** (or Aber Ac'h, in Breton) and the Aber Benoît.

Beyond Lannilis, lie **Landéda** and L'Aber Wrac'h, a seaside resort on the Baie des Anges (Angels' Bay). Nearby are the ruins of the late 15th-century convent of Our Lady of the Angels, in a truly beautiful setting. From there, go on to the **St. Marga-**ret Peninsula. There is a magnificent view extending along the coast and out to sea over the reefs and islands offshore. Archaeological digs have been carried out on **Guennoc** (or Gaignog) and the remains uncovered span a very long period stretching from the Paleolithic Age to mediaeval times.

When you get back to Lannilis, take a narrow road north-eastwards to **Kerouartz Castle** overlooking the south bank of the Aber Wrac'h. It is a fine Breton Renaissance building (1580-1602) with pedimented skylights. In front of it is a courtyard and fountain. A carved fireplace decorates the great drawing room.

The **Aber Benoît** is best seen after leaving Lannilis, from the Tréglonou Bridge on the Ploudalmézeau road.

PLOVAN
8m. NW of Pont-L'Abbé

The 16th-century **parish church** has several Romanesque arches but is less well-known than the ruins of the **Chapel of Our Lady** (or St. Guy) of **Languidou** (c.1260) for the chapel is an essential landmark in the history of Breton architecture. Some say that this was the birthplace of the so-called Pont-Croix School which drew its inspiration from the Anglo-Norman style and, throughout the 13th century, smothered Lower Cornouaille with compound pillars, slender arcading, and decorated capitals. The chapel was restored early in the 15th century. The Gothic rose window in the chevet, the credenza, and the funeral niche all date from this period.

The Chapel of Notre-Dame de Languidou.

POINTE DU RAZ
22m. W of Douarnenez

The long rocky promontory that is the Pointe du Raz in **Plogoff** descends to sea level in a series of steps. Eight miles offshore beyond the Old Lady Lighthouse (Phare de la Vieille) is the island of Sein with its circlet of reefs. The pass, or race, is one of the most dangerous in Europe.

For a walk round the headland (alt.234 ft.), you should be accompanied by an official guide. There are striking views of the sea's erosion of the rocky outcrop. The waves rush in, underwashing the crest, sinking, and frothing up in a headily-deep depression called the **"Hell of Plogoff"**, where the souls of the departed can be heard moaning. The headland is really a battlefield enduring the ceaseless assault of the waves.

Between the two headlands at each end of **Cap Sizun** lies the **Baie des Trépassés** (Bay of the Dead) which has long symbolised the point of departure for the hereafter. Tradition has it that the mortal remains of dead Druids were taken from here for burial on Sein. Every two years, on 2nd November, the drowned assemble here before setting off in search of those they once loved.

Some people believe that the **Etang de Lawal,** which lies behind a shingle bar, was the site of the town of Ys. In fact, it probably stood somewhere at the eastern end of the Baie de Douarnenez (q.v.).

Beyond is the **Pointe du Van** (alt. 211ft.), younger sister to the Pointe du Raz, a less stormy but more desolate cape. There is neither shopping centre nor car park sticking out like a sore thumb on this headland. There is only the humble **St. They's Chapel** on the heath overlooking the cliff. The hamlet of **Trouguer** to the south-east of the chapel has a Gallo-Roman wall. Above the church in **Cléden-Cap Sizun** is a 16th-century belltower. On the west wall and south porch are carvings of fishing boats.

The parish of Cléden-Cap Sizun has a **Gallic fort,** at the Pointe de Castelmeur.

Pointe du Raz.

Pointe du Van.

Top right : *Baie des Trépassés.*

Bottom right : *The chapel at Cap Sizun.*

PONT-AVEN
10m. W of Quimperlé

In the latter years of the last century, Pont-Aven was the meeting-place of the artists who were followers of Paul Gauguin; he stayed in the town on several occasions in 1886 and 1889. With Paul Sérusier, Emile Bernard, Maurice Denis, Pierre Bonnard, and Meyer de Haan, he is one of the founder members of the "Pont-Aven School". Overlooking the **Paul-Gauguin Beach** is the Gloannec Inn at which the painters used to stay. The house next door used to be the home of "Beautiful Angela" whose portrait was painted by Gauguin. On the town hall square, a plaque commemorates Miss Julia Guillou, the "good hostess" whose door was always open to the colonies of English and American artists who then frequented the town. The **Gauguin Museum** in the town hall, which is open during the tourist season, has an exhibition relating to the Pont-Aven School.

Another artist also helped to "launch" the resort - the bard and songster Théodore Botrel (1868-1925).

To the north-west at the edge of the Bois d'Amour stands the 16th-century **Trémalo Chapel.** It contains not only statues of the Madonna and Child and St. Anne but also a large Crucifix which provided the inspiration for Gauguin's "Yellow Christ".

On the Concarneau road on the outskirts of the town is **Levazen Manor,** a late 16th-century building in which Gauguin had his studio.

The calvary beside the church in **Nizon,** two miles to the north-west of Pont-Aven, is also well-known thanks to Gauguin - he painted its Pietà.

PONT-L'ABBE
11m. SW of Quimper

The capital of the Bigouden Region has remained, in some respects at least, the "quiet little town" that the writer Flaubert discovered in 1847. Yet it was scarcely as peaceful as all that, for some of the women

were involved in a fight and Flaubert, who was after all a surgeon's son, had to treat the injured! At that time, the women did not wear the tall mitre-shaped headdress that we see today; it is a 20th-century creation (the Joanne Guide still mentions a "tiny headdress" in 1914). The so-called Bigouden lacework is also a recent innovation (1902).

The town gets its name (Pont-'n-Abad in Breton) from a bridge said to have been built here by the priests of Loctudy. The community had a Carmelite convent from 1389 onwards but it was demolished in the 19th century. A 13th- and 18th-century **castle-town hall** houses the Bigouden Museum (costume, furniture, and an exhibition of life at sea). The **Church of Our Lady of Carmel** (14th and 15th centuries) has two rose windows (the one in the chevet is quite remarkable) and a nave with eight bays. **Lambour Chapel** (13th and 15th centuries) has lain in ruins since the end of the last century. The top of the tower was lost in 1675 when the Dukc de Chaulnes, who had been instructed by Louis XIV to put down the Stamped Paper Revolt, had the spire of the six churches in

Pont-L'Abbé: the castle-town hall.

the Caval headland demolished.

If you need an excuse to stroll through the town, there are a few 17th-century houses, the Bigouden Memorial (1931) by the sculptor Bazin, and a shady jetty.

In Plomeur, two miles away on the road to Saint-Jean-Trolimon is **La Tréminou Chapel,** a 15th-century building with an enormous roof. It was one of the hotbeds of revolt during the Red Bonnet Uprising.

Kernuz Castle (16th century), to the south-west of Pont-L'Abbé on the Plomeur road, still has its ramparts. The castle was restored by Joseph Bigot from 1843 onwards and is now a hotel and restaurant.

To the east of Pont-L'Abbé, the 16th-century church in **Combrit** is famous for its Renaissance tower which was rebuilt in the 18th century. Inside are carved corbels and an alabaster statue of the Holy Trinity.

On the Quimper road, just on the outskirts of Combrit, is a path leading down to **Combrit Cove,** a charming inlet of the R.Odet.

Near Pont-Aven. ▶

The gentle atmosphere of Pont-Aven. ▼

Pont-Croix: the porch at Notre-Dame de Roscudon.

PONT-CROIX
10m. SW of Douarnenez

Lying on the right bank of the Goyen, Pont-Croix (Pont-e-Kroaz, in Breton) is more or less the capital of Cap Sizun. It was once not only a busy commercial harbour but also a seat of justice and a religious centre famous for its seminarists' secondary school (formerly the Ursuline convent) whose 18th-century chapel and buildings are still standing.

The oldest parts of the **Church of Our Lady of Roscudon** ("wood pigeon hill" in Breton) date from the 13th century. Later, it was altered and completed. The late 14th-century south porch has three very unusual tall gables (one of them is larger than the others) with trefoiled and quatrefoiled openwork. The mid 15th-century belltower is topped by a **spire** 218 ft. high which was used as a model for the spires on St. Corentin's Cathedral in Quimper. At the west end of the north wall are two small doors said to have been used by lepers.

Inside, the **pillars** with their barrel vaulting (although they date from the Gothic period) are exceptionally elegant. Along with the capitals and multi-ribbed arches, they are characteristic of a quite different architectural style based on English and Welsh building techniques. There are several such churches in Lower Cornouaille; indeed, they are described as belonging to the Pont-Croix School (cf.Plovan). A **carving of the Last Supper** (17th century) is of Flemish inspiration.

PORSPODER
17m. NW of Brest

Porspoder is basically a seaside resort whose attraction lies in the rugged coastline that is constantly being reshaped by the waves. There are a large number of creeks in the area, each with its tiny beach of sand or shingle. After dark, the lamps from the lighthouses offer an almost unreal spectacle. The **Pointe du Garchine** is a good vantage point.

Porspoder Church is not old (despite its 18th-century tower) but it does overlook the shore. A stained glass window serves as a reminder of the legend of how Bude arrived in Porspoder in the 6th century seated on a floating stone.

Larret, two miles south-east of Porspoder, is a charming village with a small 14th-century chapel half-hidden by the overhanging branches of beech trees. On the road to Larret is the Kerouezel menhir (22 ft. tall). But the nearby **Kergadiou menhirs** are of greater interest. The one now lying on the ground is 36 ft. long; the other one, which is still upright, measures 29 ft.

Melon, two miles to the south, is a seaweed-gathering port situated on a rugged and bare stretch of coastline. **L'Aber-Ildut** further south is another small harbour. It has a top-quality granite quarry which provided the stone for the base of the obelisk on the Place de la Concorde in Paris.

The religious procession at Penhors.

PORTSALL-KERSAINT
17m. NW of Brest

The twin resorts of Portsall and Kersaint attract many families during the holiday season, and it is true that the area is both quiet and picturesque. The coastroad from Portsall south to Lanildut affords some magnificent seaviews (e.g. at the **Pointe de Landunvez**). There is another attractive view of the coastline from the **Pointe de Guilligui,** on which are the remains of a passage grave.

From the charming harbour of Portsall, you can see the **Portsall Rocks** to the north-west and the **Ile Verte** closer to shore. It was just opposite the Pozguen Dunes that the supertanker ''Amoco Cadiz'' foundered in March 1978.

In Kersaint, there is the admirable **Chapel of Our Lady of Assistance** (16th century with later alterations), standing in a rustic setting. The stained glass windows tell the story of St. Tanguy, the founder of the monastery on the nearby Pointe Saint-Mathieu. There is a very rare ossuary with niches.

Not far away is the 13th-century **Trémazan Castle,** now in ruins. All that remains is the keep, one wall and a doorway.

POULDREUZIC
13m. W of Quimper

Since 1907, Pouldreuzic has been Hénaff country (the company had 175 employees in 1987... and it produces 140,000 tins of pâté per day). Since 1975, it has also been known as the setting for the tales in Pierre Jakez Hélias' ''Horse of Pride'' (the author was born in 1914). Readers can try to rediscover the book's atmosphere near the **Chapel of Our Lady of Penhors** (16th century with a few 13th-century features). The author regales us with inside stories of the procession held at the chapel in September.

St. Paban's Church in **Lababan** is an attractive place of worship (15th-16th centuries, with late 13th-century arcading). To the south-east on the Tréogat road is **Lesnavor Manor** (16th century). Peumérit, further east, has a number of castles or manorhouses - Lesmadec (16th century), Penquelennec (15th century), and Prat-ar-Stang whose remains are said to date from the 11th century. The church has a 13th-century chancel and a stained glass window made in 1539.

Penhors : the torchlight procession. ▶

Le Pouldu.　　　　　　　　　　　　　　　　　　　　　　　*Pointe de Primel.* ▶

LE POULDU
8m. S of Quimperlé, in Clohars-Carnoët

Le Pouldu, which like Dublin means "black pond" lies at the mouth of the R.Laïta. It has become `a traditional seaside resort. It had its moment of glory in 1889 when Paul Gauguin stayed here with the Dutchman, Meyer de Hann. The town has a few memories of the artist.

The Chapel of Our Lady of Peace (15th and 17th centuries) was once St.Maudé's Chapel in Nizun but it was transferred in 1959. The modern stained glass windows are by Jean Le Moal and Alfred Manessier. The chapel has an interesting rood-beam.

Four miles north of Le Pouldu are the remains of the **Abbey of St.Maurice of Carnoët** in a beautiful setting at the edge of a forest on the right bank of the R.Laïta. The abbey founded in 1177 has now disappeared except for the 13th-century chapter house.

POINTE DE PRIMEL
13m. N of Morlaix, in Plougasnou

Coming from Morlaix or Lannion, you arrive in Plougasnou (q.v.) on the D.46 which carries on to **Primel-Trégastel,** a busy seaside resort. The road down to the coast is magnificent. There are rocks on all sides and the reefs run far out to sea. The Pointe de Primel seems unwilling to leave terra firma. It is an irregular shape and there are piles of rocks that are suddenly separated so that the tip forms an isthmus, especially at high tide. The rocks, which are darker than the ones on the Pink Granite Coast, have a singular auburn or reddish tinge. In fine weather, there is a panoramic view from one of the headlands.

Back on the Morlaix road, take the 'B' road (the "départementale") that follows the coast half-a-mile from Primel. The shore dips inward to form the cove at **Le Diben.**

PRIMELIN
8m. W of Pont-Croix

It is in Primelin to the west of Audierne that you can see the finest sanctuary in the whole Sizun peninsula, **St.Tujen's Chapel.** Built by the lords of Lézurec who lived in a nearby manor, the chapel is Flamboyant Gothic in style (16th century). The 91-foot tower is based on the one in Quimper. In the middle of the south wall is a 17th-century statue of St.Tujen holding a key. Inside, the altar in the south arm of the transept is Renaissance; at the corner is a statue of St.John Discalceat. The remarkable baptistry (1674) is decorated with painted panelling dating from 1705. The **catafalque** (1642) shows Adam and Eve. The Our Lady of Grace reredos was made in 1694.

People used to pray to Tujen, a monk from across the Channel who became Abbot of Daoulas, for protection from rabies, called "droug sant Tujen" in Breton.

◄ *Quimper : a general view.*

QUIMPER
48m. S of Brest

The capital of Cornouaille is one of Brittany's brightest gems, set in a beautiful ring of hills and dales. This "charming little place", as Flaubert put it, lies a few miles inland from the sea at the confluence of the rivers Steir, Jed and Odet, hence its Breton name - Kemper.

Legend has it that King Gradlon was the town's founder. After his daughter, Dahud, had opened the sluices which protected the town of Ys from the ocean (cf. Douarnenez), Gradlon fell back on Quimper where he was crowned King of Cornouaille. He introduced vineyards to the region and appointed Corentin, the hermit with the miraculous fish, first Bishop of Quimper.

St.Corentin's Cathedral stands on the site of a former Romanesque church, and its construction lasted from the 13th to the 19th centuries. Its spires, for example, (designed by Joseph Bigot) were built in 1855 and were inspired by the ones in Pont-Croix. The twin towers (mid 15th century) were part of the Anglo-Norman tradition that was so widespread in Brittany. The equestrian statue of King Gradlon (1858) on the platform was based on an earlier statue that was destroyed by revolutionaries in 1793. Only one doorway escaped damage during the French Revolution, St.Catherine's Door (15th century) next to the Bishop's Palace.

Although relatively small (299 ft. in length), the cathedral is a fine example of Gothic architecture as developed in Brittany. The great spans with their luxurious moulding are evidence of the influence exerted by Normandy's architects. The chancel (c.1285) is not in line with the nave, probably because the builders were anxious to incorporate the Victory Chapel in the 13th-century sanctuary. The vaulting in the chancel dates from the 15th century. Despite successive waves of destruction, there are still some 15th-century stained glass windows (they have been restored).

The remains of the **ramparts** beside the cathedral indicate that this was once a walled town.

The old Bishop's Palace built by the Rohan family in 1508 (beside the cathedral) is still an impressive building despite restoration. It houses the **Breton Museum** which has some remarkable exhibits.

Not far from the cathedral is the **St.Francis covered market** (designed by the architects Bizouarn, Lachaud and Le Berre). It is a convincing example of contemporary architecture (the rafters have the shape of an upturned hull).

On the other side of the square, the delightful **Art Gallery** (1872) is of major interest. It has paintings, sketches and engravings from the 16th to 20th centuries.

A stroll through old Quimper should not be confined to the **Rue Kéréon** (i.e. Shoemaker's Street) opposite the cathedral. You really have to wander at will, for the town has more atmosphere than specific

Old Quimper.

tourist attractions. Go into the labyrinth of streets and squares that bear such evocative names e.g. Place au Beurre (Butter Square), Rue des Boucheries (the Shambles), or Rue des Gentilhommes (Gentlemen's Street). In the **Rue du Guéaudet** (from the Breton "keodet" meaning "a city"), the "house of heads" is said to show some of the pickpockets of the day. The narrow Venelle St.Nicolas has a flight of steps halfway up it. The finest house in Quimper stands in the **Rue du Sallé** ("Le Minuellou"). With its corbels, beams and carved fireplaces, it is a masterpiece of architecture - and restoration.

The **Rue Kéréon** leads to the **Terre-au-Duc** (literally "Duke's Land") which, unlike the town within the walls (episcopal land) was governed by the Dukes of Brittany.

At the foot of **Mount Frugy** (which towers some 227 ft. above the town), the **Allées de Locmaria** lead to the suburb of the same name, stronghold of the local glazed earthenware industry. In 1690, a ceramics expert from Provence, J-B. Bousquet, settled in Locmaria. There is a **Faïence Museum** on the Bénodet road, and the Kéraluc potteries (Rue de la Troménie) are also open to the public. It is at the foot of Mount Frugy that the Folklore Festival of Cornouaille is held every July.

Notre-Dame Church is the oldest monument in Quimper. The Romanesque nave dates from the first half of the 11th century; the chancel, transept and tower are 12th century. This Romanesque sanctuary replaced a Carolingian church of which a few traces still remain.

Five miles out of town on the Coray road to the north-east are the **Stangala Rocks** ("Ely's pond"), half hidden in a gorge where the R.Odet disappears amidst the undergrowth.

QUIMPERLE
30m. E of Quimper

It is in Quimperlé, in the narrow valley with steeply-sloping sides, that the R.Laïta is formed by the confluence of the Isole and Ellé. The town's name, in fact, is based on its geographical situation (Kemper Elle means "the confluence of the Ellé").

In the **lower town** near the Place Nationale are the buildings of the former **Holy Cross Abbey** (17th century), now used for more mundane purposes. From the cloisters, you can see **Holy Cross Church,** the former minster, which is a gem of Romanesque architecture. It was built in 1083 but had to be rebuilt in the 19th century when the central tower collapsed, almost totally destroying the church. Restoration work (1864-1868) was carried out with the utmost care and attention (some even say with too much care) and recreated the church as it once was. It is built to a circular layout similar to the Holy Sepulchre in Jerusalem. It has a rotunda onto which open a porch and three apsidal chapels. The apse has withstood the test of time and is probably the finest of its kind in Brittany, with its windows, arcatures, pillars and capitals. The 11th-century crypt is still intact; its capitals, decorated like the ones in the chancel, are quite remarkable.

Opposite the church is the **Rue de Brémond-d'Ars** (old houses). Across from the ruins of St.Colomba's Church is the **Rue Dom-Maurice** (timbered houses).

To get to the **upper town,** take either the Rue Savary or one of a number of flights of steps. The **Church of Our Lady of the Assumption and St.Michael** immediately catches the eye. The nave is 13th century and the chancel slightly more recent (15th century). Above it is a large square tower which lost its lead spire during the French Revolution when it was melted down to make bullets.

The discreet charms of Quimperlé. ▶

The Romanesque crypt in Sainte-Croix in Quimperlé. ▼

LE RELECQ

10m. S of Morlaix, in Plounéour-Ménez

The former **abbey** of Our Lady of Le Relecq, which was built in the Monts d'Arrée, was one of the centres of Cistercian Brittany. Historically, its existence dates from 1132 but legend has it that it existed in the 6th century.

The French Revolution dealt the abbey a death blow. Its last prior gave up the frock and became sub-prefect of Lure (Haute-Saône in Central France) in 1800. All that remains of the great Romanesque Cistercian abbey, which has been partially restored, are a few buildings, the entrance gate, a **fountain** with an obelisk (17th century) and a couple of lakes. Inside the church is the staircase leading to the monks' dorter, and the Romanesque **capitals** with motifs stylised until they become geometrical shapes. In the summer, the place is used for festivals and cultural events.

LA ROCHE-MAURICE

3m. E of Landerneau

A vulture's nest at the top of a mountain. That was Flaubert's description of the castle of La Roche-Maurice (13th-14th centuries) of which only ruins remain. But the setting is superb. Coming from the dual carriageway, the road crosses the R.Elorn and, beyond the level crossing on the Paris-Brest line, climbs upwards providing visitors with beautiful views of the Elorn valley. The trip is especially recommended at sunset.

The village of La Roche-Maurice ("Ar Roc'h-Morvan", in Breton) straddling an outcrop of rock (alt. 162 ft.), has the splendour of its 16th-century parish close to offer visitors. The outside of St. Yves' Church is particularly noteworthy for its tower; the double bellchamber is topped by a typical Cornouaille spire. The richly-decorated south porch leads into the church, which still has a finely-carved 16th-century **rood-screen.** The twelve

La Roche-Maurice : the parish close. ▲

The church in La Roche-Maurice : the rood-screen. ▶

Apostles are depicted above caryatids adorned with grotesque figures. At the end of the chancel is the outstanding **Passion Window** (1539) which influenced much of the region's stained glass work.

The main façade of the **ossuary** (1639-1640) is Classical in design, with Corinthian columns and pilasters. A sort of **Danse Macabre** is carved above the stoup and a skeleton warns his "fellow humans", "I kill you all".

You may also like to visit the ruined chapel of **Pont-Christ** (1533) to the north-east of La Roche-Maurice.

ROSCOFF
3m. N of Saint-Pol-de-Léon

Listen to what Julien Gracq wrote in 1980 : "The element that is missing in "Amour Jaunes" by Corbière and that I am so fond of, is the gentle atmosphere that is particular to Roscoff. There are few places in which the solitary dinner hour on beaches emptied of people, when the sun is still quite high in the heavens, seemed as delicious and intimate for the late stroller, as tender both in colour and stillness, between the sky that is slowly turning yellow just above the horizon and the slate blue of the sea. Just as, along its paths, the soft green grass is as muted and furry as an almond husk".

The "gentle atmosphere that is particular to Roscoff" is undeniable, and it explains how a Mediterranean type of vegetation has been able to thrive on this "blacksmith's hill" (apparently the meaning of the name Roscoff) that has become a major ferry terminal with Brittany Ferries' sailings to England and Ireland. Roscoff has always had a sea-based economy. Whereas Saint-Pol sends early vegetables (artichokes, cauliflowers, and potatoes) to the rest of France and to Germany, Roscoff exports the produce overseas. The town even has old sailors who specialised in the sale of onions throughout Britain, the "Onion Johnnies" who pedalled all over the United Kingdom, going right up to Scotland, and who later came back to Roscoff to enjoy their retirement. The tradition dates back to 1828.

Roscoff, then, is a **port,** or to be more precise a series of ports - the ferry terminal (1974) at the Pointe de Bloscon on the east coast, the old harbour nearer the town, and the new harbour (lobsters, crayfish, and, formerly, coastal trade). It is also

The harbour in Roscoff.

An aerial view of Roscoff.

from here that boats leave for the island of Batz.

The old **walls** which once protected Roscoff from the sea are now well inland. At the corner of the ramparts near the harbour, there is a 16th-century watchtower known as Mary Stuart's Turret.

The Church of Our Lady of Croaz-Baz dates from the mid 16th century. Its lanterned belltower (late 16th century) is particularly worthy of note.

There are numerous walks in the Roscoff area, especially to the west where visitors can take a stroll to the beaches and the **Pointe de Perharidy** (a physiotherapy centre that uses the sun and the sea to treat children with motor disabilities). Roscoff's climate is beneficial in the curing of certain illnesses, e.g. bone tuberculosis, and the seawater is used in both thalassotherapy and sea kelp baths.

ROSPORDEN
14m. E of Quimper

For many people, Rosporden is an overnight stop at the junction of several major roads and it is a pleasant place to drop anchor. It is hardly surprising that the town has become famous for its good food. While your digestion is at work, try going for a stroll round the **small lakes.**

Rosporden is also the capital of mead, known locally as "chouchenn", which is made from water and fermented honey (at present the honey is imported from Eastern Europe, Italy and Spain). And if you're suffering from flu, don't bother your doctor; just have a large cup of mead gently warmed over a low heat.

For those in search of more spiritual nourishment, there is the **church** (14th-17th centuries) whose typical mid 14th-century tower is reflected in the waters of a lake. The porch is also 14th century. Inside, there is a 15th-century Madonna and Child, a carved gilded High Altar (17th century) and a statue of Christ being laid in the tomb.

ISLAND OF SEIN
Off Plogoff

The landscape is bare, the ground flat, the vegetation stunted. The writer Henri Queffélec made the island famous by his novel, "Un recteur de l'île de Sein" (pub. 1945), on which the film "Dieu a besoin des hommes" was based.

The average altitude scarcely exceeds 5 ft. which explains why Sein was almost submerged on several occasions (1830, 1868, and 1897). In 1820, the island was 2m. long and 975 yds. wide; today, it is 1 1/2 m. long and only 866 yds. wide.

Sein has been sanctified by myth and legend. Over the centuries, it has been thought to be the Roman Insula Sena on which nine priestesses worshipped their gods, or the Island of the Seven Sleeps, the burial ground of the Druids. Of course, the souls of the departed (the Anaon) wander near Sein.

To visit the island, go where the will takes you. The alleys round the harbour sometimes have strange names (the Street of the Impudent Cockerel, or Go-up-to-heaven Street). They are not more than a yard or two wide.

After an outbreak of cholera in 1885, the local women decided to wear the "jobelinenn", or widow's headdress.

A memorial to the Free People of Sein sculpted by René Quillivic stands between the two halves of the island. It serves as a reminder that at the end of June 1940, almost 150 islanders set sail for Britain.

From the top of the lighthouse on the western side of the island, there is a view across the **Sein Causeway,** a line of reefs that run some 6 miles out to sea. At the tip is the Ar-Men Lighthouse, one of the most inhospitable on the coast. It took almost 15 years to complete (1867-1881).

The island of Sein. (Photo J.-P. Prével)

Sizun : the parish close.

SIZUN
20m. SW of Morlaix

The little town of Sizun on one of the banks of the R.Elorn has slate-hung houses and an outstanding parish close.

The masterpiece is probably the **triumphal gateway** (1588-1590). It is quite unique and comprises three semicircular arches. The platform, with its balustrade and lantern-turrets, stands on Corinthian columns. Above it is an altar and calvary. It is an astonishing piece of architecture displaying both power and elegance ; it is much more reminiscent of the triumphal arches built by the Romans than of Finistère's closes (cf. Berven).

The **ossuary** (1585-1588), which is also very carefully designed and executed, has two levels. The upper section shows the Apostles on guard in niches separated by fluted pilasters. Lower down are small semicircular windows between which are caryatids representing rather whimsical people.

The octagonal spire (1723-1735), some 195 ft. high, on the 16th- to 18th-century **St. Sullian's Church** is not unlike the Kreizkêr in Saint-Pol. The great Flamboyant Gothic porch dates from the 16th century. The apse is decorated with a carved frieze (1661). Inside the church, note the numerous altars and reredos (17th century), two of which (one made of stone, the other of wood) flank the chancel. Or you may prefer some of the statues or, more outstanding still, the **wood panelling** and corbels.

St. Pitère's Church in **Tréhou** to the south-west of Sizun dates mainly from the 17th century. The calvary was erected in 1578. Hundreds of Bronze Age axes have been uncovered in the vicinity.

SPEZET
10m. SW of Carhaix-Plouguer

The **Chapel of Our Lady of Le Crann** is one of the few rural churches to have kept its original furnishings and, more importantly, its stained glass windows. On top of the building (1532-1535) is a Renaissance lantern-turret which can be reached from the outside by a flight of steps cut into the pitch of the roof. The **stained glass windows** (1545-1550) show German (Rhineland) and Italian influences. In addition to Christ's Passion, they depict Jesus' childhood and the stories of St. James, St. Ely (patron saint of blacksmiths) and St. Lawrence (based on an engraving by the Italian artist, Marcantonio Raimondi). Panelled reredos surround the High Altar.

All along the **Aulne Canal** runs a towpath that constitutes one of the best walks in the neighbourhood. To the east of Spézet, the little **Cudel** road leads south to one of the vantage points in the Montagnes Noires (q.v.), the **Roc'h Art Werc'hez** (the Virgin Mary's Rock). Toul-Laeron lies within the boundary of Spézet.

SAINT-HERBOT
19m. NE of Châteaulin, in Plonévez-du-Faou

St. Herbot, patron saint of horned animals (as is his colleague, St. Cornély), has given his name to this hamlet not far from Loqueffret, lying in a wooded corrie on the southern slopes of the Monts d'Arrée. Not long ago, local farmers still used to process to a stone table on which they would lay a tuft of hair from the tails of their cows and oxen, in order to ensure the protection of the veterinary saint who is regarded with

much reverence thoughout Brittany.

The Gothic **chapel** (14th-16th centuries) has an elegant square tower with balustrades, based on the ones on St. Corentin's Cathedral in Quimper. The main portal (1516) is a fine piece of architecture ; it has a double basket-handle door. On the north side, a flight of steps leads up to a 14th-century door. Painted statues of the Apostles welcome visitors in the south porch (1498). Nearby, on a beech-lined esplanade, is a **Cross** with carved figures (1571) made of kersantite. The buttresses on the chevet of the chapel are decorated with Renaissance lantern-turrets topped by the crescent moon (cf.Kerjean Castle). There is an adjoining ossuary (1588) at the corner of the south porch.

Inside is a fine set of decorative furnishings including a pulpitum

ornamented with colonnades and a frieze of carved panels (16th century). On each side of the pulpitum are the stone tables on which the farmers used to lay their offerings. Note also the 15 choir stalls and the Passion Window (1566). St. Herbot lies buried in one of the tombs.

One mile to the north-east is the former **Rusquec Castle** (16th century), now a farm. From there, you can go to the **Saint-Herbot Dam,** built in 1929 in the narrow Ellez Valley. The landscape is wild but grandiose with a rock fall on the valley floor.

Loqueffret, just over two miles to the west of Saint-Herbot, lies at a crossroads. The roads north and south lead from Morlaix to Châteauneuf-du-Faou and Quimperlé, while east and west they run from Huelgoat to Pleyben. This means that Loqueffret has a lot of

Notre-Dame de Crann : mid 16th-century stained glass windows.

The calvary and church in Saint-Hernin.

◀ *Saint-Herbot : the Pietà* (photo by H. Champollion).

through traffic but that people seldom stop there, which is a pity. The church has a number of objects of interest (16th-17th centuries) e.g. statues, carvings still with some of their original paintwork, several reredos and a gallery.

SAINT-HERNIN
6m. SW of Carhaix

The 16th-17th century church, decorated with corbels bearing masks, is built in the shape of the Greek letter 'tau', a fairly common layout in inland Finistère. The 16th-century calvary has three Crosses. On the main shaft is a statue of St. Michael slaying the dragon, while to each side are the thieves writhing in agony. The church and **calvary** form a harmonious set of buildings, with the ossuary dating from 1697.

Just over a mile to the east on the Port-de-Carhaix road, the **Kerbreuder calvary** is, along with the one in Tronoën, the oldest in Brittany (15th century). In both cases, the thieves are shown on the shaft of the calvary, which is very unusual. The calvary here has a strange central niche. Although in a poor state of repair (the Crosses are not original), it displays scenes from the Bible with a certain vigour.

SAINT-JEAN-DU-DOIGT
10m. N of Morlaix

At one time, the most astonishing events occurred in Brittany, for example in 1437 when a young man from the nearby village of Plougasnou came to give the parish John the Baptist's index finger which he had

just discovered, miraculously.

The parish soon took the name of Sant-Yann-ar-Biz ("ar Biz" means "the finger" in Breton). It was a shrewd business move, for the relic has curative powers which attract crowds of pilgrims every year, at the Feast of St. John. On this particular day, tradition demands that the afflicted should wash their face with water from a fountain with several superimposed basins, known as "The Pump". The Italianate **fountain** (1690) is decorated with figures.

Part of the Flamboyant Gothic **church** dates from the 15th century - the West Front (except the door which was built in 1512), the first two spans in the nave and the south aisle, and the north aisle. The remainder of the church is 16th century.

Pointe Saint-Mathieu.

POINTE SAINT-MATHIEU
16m. W of Brest, in Plougonvelin.

Less westerly than the Pointe de Corsen (cf.Plouarzel), the Pointe Saint-Mathieu (or Penn-ar-Bed in Breton i.e. "land's end") attracts a far greater number of visitors because it is easier to reach from Brest. Moreover, it has to be admitted that the view is impressive. From the top of the 520 ft. **lighthouse**, it stretches to the Vieux-Moines reefs that seem to be scattered at random like pieces of flotsam, to the Pierres-Noires Causeway, and to the islands of Béniguet, Molène and Ushant.

-Southwards the view encompasses the entrance to Brest harbour, the Crozon Peninsula, and even (on fine days) the island of Sein and the Pointe du Raz. The lighthouse itself is very modern, and it has a range of 37 miles.

On the edge of the cliffs stands the memorial to the sailors lost during the First World War. It is a sculpture by René Quillivic, representing a Breton woman.

Saint-Mathieu used to be quite a large town, and a monastery was founded here by St. Tanguy in the 6th century.

The **abbey church** lies in ruins but you can still see the impressive 13th-century chancel which is similar to the one in Saint-Malo, with the thick walls and the flat chevet that are typical of great Breton cathedrals. There is also a tower. The side aisles date from the 16th century. The **Chapel of Our Lady of Grace,** which was restored just over a century ago, has a 14th-century door, all that remains of the old parish church.

On the Plougonvelin road to the east are two Christianised steles with the curious name of the "Monks' Gibbet".

SAINT-POL-DE-LEON
10m. NW of Morlaix.

The town gets its name (Kastell-Paol, in Breton) from St. Pol-Aurélien, a Welsh monk who brought Christianity to Armorica in the 6th century. He is often mentioned in this region, especially on Ushant and Batz. As a great slayer of dangerous beasts, he put an end to the deeds of a dragon. The town of Saint-Pol is also the "artichoke capital". The plant was first imported from Italy in the 15th century (the word "artichoke" comes directly from a dialect word in Lombardy).

The best way of discovering the town is to stroll through its streets and alleyways. On the **Place du Petit-Cloître** is a prebend's house (1530) that was once the residence of the cathedral's canons. There is another prebend's house at no.2 Rue de la Rosière. The main road in the town is the **Rue Leclerc,** which runs from the cathedral to the Kreizkêr. There are several old houses in it. Take a look up at the dormer windows. On some of the buildings there are particularly ornate (no.30 dates from 1680, no.12 is a Renaissance building, and nos.9 and 31 are also worthy of attention).

There are a large number of churches and chapels in the town. First of all, tere is **St. Fiacre's Chapel** in the cemetery. It is a 15th-century building with a Flamboyant Gothic belltower (although the campanile is 18th century). The **Chapel of Our Lady of Kreizkêr** ("Kreizkêr" means "town centre") is a 14th- and 15th-century sanctuary which may be of English inspiration. Although the nave is tall, the overall dimensions of the chapel are fairly modest. It is the spire, based on St. Peter's in Caen, which elicits admiration.

If you go along the Rue Leclerc, you will reach the large Place du Guébriand, where a bustling market takes place every Tuesday. There is a view of the south side of the cathedral with the porch and the south arm of the transept containing the great rose window. Go round the cathedral towards the two mighty towers; they are not as tall on the one on the Kreizkêr but they nevertheless stand over 160 ft. high. To the north are the buildings of the former Bishop's Palace (18th century) but the see was transferred to Quimper in 1790. The building now houses the town hall.

Visitors enter the cathedral by the porch on the West Front (to the right is the so-called Kakouz Door which was reserved for lepers) and are always struck by the length of the nave compared to its constricted width. The pale stone in Caen limestone (teh rest is granite).

An aerial view of Saint-Pol-de-Léon.

de Bescond from Carhaix. The decoration on the façade is an outstanding example of Breton Renaissance architecture (ribbed pediment, arched doorway and windows, Corinthian capitals, shelled niches, and lantern-turrets). Inside, in the crypt, is a statue of Christ being laid in the tomb (c.1699) comprising life-sized painted figures. This striking piece of sculpture was the work of Jacques Lespagnol from Morlaix. Today, the chapel is the **treasure house.**

A Renaissance porch (1625) leads into the **church.** The ringed pillars are copies of the ones designed for the Tuileries by Philibert Delorme from Lyons who had been greatly influenced by the Italian Renaissance. The belltower (1599-1610) is based on the one in Pleyben on which work had started some years earlier. It has a proud Renaissance outline and is topped by a dome. The belltower on the west gable-end is the oldest part of the church, dating from 1563.

The interior is somewhat disappointing, but it should be said that both nave and chancel were altered in the early 18th century. The furnishings, however, are representative of the Counter-Reformation and are quite remarkable. The **pulpit** is worth a close look; it dates from 1683 and 1722. On the panels are the four evangelists while on the back God is shown giving Moses the tables of the Ten Commandments. The 18th-century tester is decorated with cherubs and on the top is an angel blowing the Trumpet of the Last Judgement. The decoration was influenced by the sculptors from Brest Arsenal.

The **Rosary Reredos** (1697) depicts a variety of scenes including St. Dominic and St. Catherine receiving the Rosary. The **organ** at the end of the nave is in a very high loft. The console and most of the pipes date from 1670 and were built by Jacques Mascard, an organ-builder from Landerneau who was a followed and imitator of Dallam.

Eastward from Saint-Pol is the harbour and the bay of **Pempoul,** while to the west is **Santec,** a large village with a population of approx. 2,000. **Dossen** (meaning "a hill") is a hamlet nestling among the sand dunes. From here, you can walk across to the island of **Sieck** which is a peninsula at low tide. It is half-a-mile long and has very few inhabitants. It is, in fact, Dossen's harbour.

SAINT-THEGONNEC
8m. SW of Morlaix.

The entrance to the close is a majestic **triumphal gateway** (1587) of four granite piles topped by lantern-turrets. The **calvary** (1610) was the last of the great calvaries in the Léon Region. It has a plain base and three Crosses (the one in the centre, which bears a plethora of carvings of people, angels and horsemen, has two crossbars). The Passion procession shows numerous people dressed in the costume of Henri IV's day; it is an "instructive" piece of sculpture designed to make a deep impression on the faithful.

Nearby is the **funeral chapel** (or ossuary). It was built between 1676 and 1682 by the workshop of Jean

SAINTE-ANNE-LA-PALUD
16m. NW of Quimper,
in Plonévez-Porzay.

It was on this sandy beach in 1856 that the Breton sailor, Jean-Marie Le Bris, got off the ground in his home-made glider. Drawn by a galloping horse, he managed to fly some 217 yds. at a height of 325 ft. in the teeth of a gale. There is a memorial to his feat.

In the midst of desolate, undula-ting countryside 450 yds. from the beach stands **St. Anne's Chapel** built in the Neobreton Gothic style (19th century). It is here that a great reli-gious procession is held every year, during the last weekend in August.

The circular St. Barbara's **stele** in Ploëven to the north-east is 11ft. tall. Note, too, the fine **Pietà** on the cal-vary in Ploëven.

TREGUENNEC
14m. SW of Quimper.

The marsh beside the Baie d'Audierne has kept its wild, lonely, desolate atmosphere. Halfway be-tween Penhors and La Torche, Tré-guennec is a good starting-point from which to explore this stretch of land, the only one of its kind in Brittany.

The 16th-century **church** is worth a visit for its Passion Window (16th century), its carved corbels, its font decorated with a 15th-century carv-ing of the Baptism of Christ, and its 16th- and 17th-century statues including a remarkable Pietà.

Further along the D.156 road is the beach, a huge crescent stretching from Pouldreuzic to Penmarc'h. Rollers crash onto a shore that seems to extend into infinity. A shingle bar ("ar vilienn vraz", or "the large peb-bles") separates the sea from the marshy melancholy hinterland.

Trunvel Lake to the north is one of the best places in Brittany for bird-watching. Some twenty diffe-rent species come here to nest, and there are over thirty winter residents.

A road leads south-west from the village to **St. Vio's Chapel** (15th cen-tury), a tiny sanctuary nestling in its close surrounded by dry-stone walls.

The religious procession at
Sainte-Anne-la-Palud.

The Château de Trévarez.

TREVAREZ

3m. S of Châteauneuf-du-Faou, in Saint-Goazec.

The grounds at Trévarez.

At the edge of the Laz Forest (q.v.) is the remarkable **Trévarez Estate** (180 hectares) which was purchased by the county in 1968. It comprises :

— the old manor house (and 106 hectares of land) which has made into an experimental farm.

— the new castle built between 1894 and 1906 on a rock overlooking the Aulne Valley. The Neogothic design is based on the castle in Courances (Essonne). During the last war, it was used as a Rest and Recuperation Centre for German and Japanese submariners. On 6th August 1944, it was the target of a RAF air raid, and was later ransacked and pillaged. It is presently undergoing restoration.

The 75-hectare park has an extensive forest and almost 8 miles of footpaths and avenues. Nearly 300 species of rhododendrons, camelias, azaleas, and hydrangeas make up an outstanding collection of flowering shrubs. In the **archaeological museum** at the end of the luxurious stable block, are exhibits relating to recent discoveries made at Saint-Thois and Saint-Goazec. The castle houses a variety of events right through the year.

124

The calvary at Tronoën.

TRONOEN

17m. SW of Quimper, in Saint-Jean-Trolimon.

"Imagine", wrote Henri Waquet, "at the edge of wild but fertile country, a regular undulating dune covered with stubbly grass sloping down to the sea. Dotted here and there are low grey cottages. A tall chapel, dedicated to the Virgin Mary, stands nervously overlooking the landscape, topped by a central traceried tower and two small spires."

The "cathedral of the dunes" is thought to date from c.1465. Outside, note the two decorated doorways in the south wall and the rose window in the apse. Tronoën is one of the few Breton chapels to have a stone-vaulted roof.

Yet Tronoën's real masterpiece is not the church but the carved **calvary,** arguably the oldest in Brittany along with the one in Kerbreuder (cf. Saint-Hernin). The two-storeyed block of granite has "naive" figures to stimulate your imagination or your admiration. The statues, which are emotionally moving in their very closeness, have been telling the story of the birth, life, and death of Jesus for the past five hundred years (only Christ's Burial is missing). Above the rectangular base is Christ's Cross (the angels are shown collecting the Saviour's Blood) and the thieves' gibbets. The oldest part of the calvary is said to be the **Nativity;** Joseph is depicted fast asleep and the Virgin Mary is lying down.

Tronoën was built near a Roman villa, which itself stood on the site of a Gallic house. **St. Urnel's necropolis** in Plomeur is a Dark Age cemetery where, over a period of some 500 years (5th-10th centuries), more than 4,000 people were buried.

The Chapel of Beuzec-Cap Caval to the east of Tronoën is in a bad state of disrepair (all that remains of the original building is the chancel). Inside, among the stumps of statues is the 15th-century tomb of the Lord of Lestiala. The calvary outside has a skull carved on the west side, which is very unusual. The chapel has taken the old name of the Bigouden region as kept alive in Penmarc'h (q.v.).

BRIEF BIBLIOGRAPHY

BROSSE (J.), editor. - *Dictionnaire des églises de France,* vol. IV, Laffont, 1968.

CHARDRONNET (J.) - *Histoire de la Bretagne,* Nouvelles Editions Latines, 1965.

DERRIEN (P.) - *Art gothique en Bretagne,* Ouest-France, 1982.

DERRIEN (P.) - *Saint-Thégonnec,* Ouest-France, 1979.

DILASSER (M.) - *Locronan,* Ouest-France, 1981.

DUIGOU (S.) - *Les Chapelles du pays bigouden,* Ouest-France, 1976.

DUIGOU (S.) - *Le Pays de l'Odet,* Ouest-France, 1981.

GISSEROT (J.-P.) - *Brest,* Ouest-France, 1978.

GRAND (R.) - *L'Art roman en Bretagne,* A. et J. Picard, 1958.

MONMARCHE (G.) - *Bretagne, Guide Bleu,* Hachette, 1972.

MUSSAT (A.) - *Arts et culture de Bretagne : un millénaire,* Berger-Levrault, 1979.

OGEE (J.-B.), MARTEVILLE (A.), and VARIN (P.) - *Dictionnaire historique et géographique de la province de Bretagne,* 2nd Edition, Molliex, Rennes, 1843 ; reprinted 1979 by Joseph Floch, Mayenne.

PELLETIER (Y.) - *Les enclos paroissiaux,* Ouest-France, 1981.

ROYER (E.) - *Nouveau guide des calvaires bretons,* Ouest-France, 1985.

SIMON (M.) - *Landévennec,* Ouest-France, 1985.

TRIQUET (J.) - *Pointe du Raz, île de Sein,* Ouest-France, 1979.

VALLAUX (C.), WAQUET (H.), DUPOUY (A.), and CHASSE (C.) - *Visages de la Bretagne,* Horizons de France, 1941.

WAQUET (H.) - *L'art breton,* 2 vols., Arthaud, Grenoble, 1933.

A more comprehensive bibliography was published in **A New Guide to Brittany** (Ouest-France, 1984).

A tiny chapel lost in the depths of the country near Trévarez.

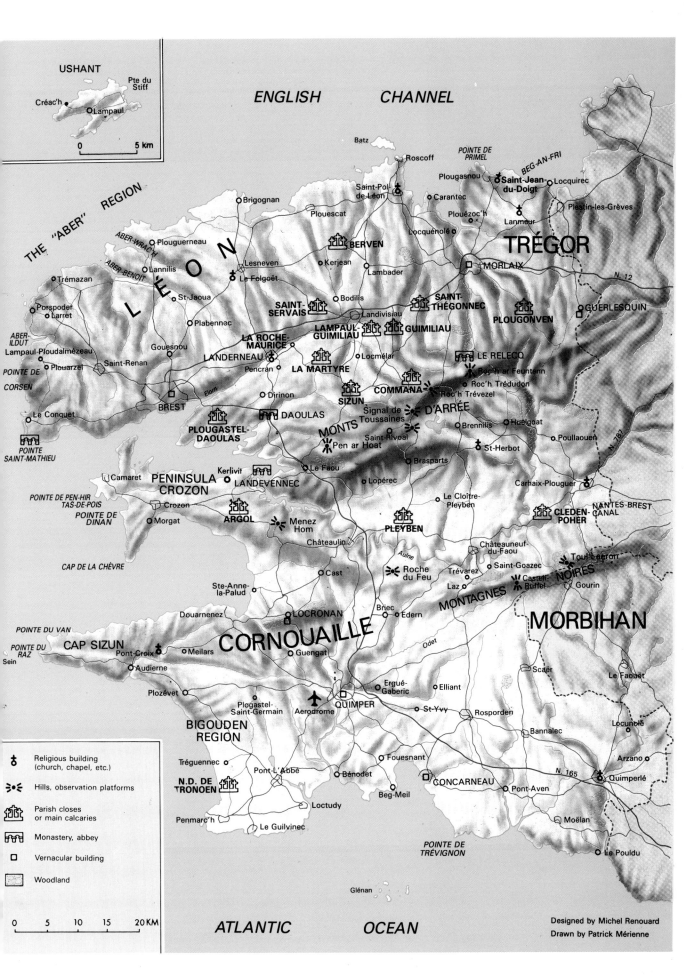

ENGLISH CHANNEL

USHANT

Créac'h
Lampaul
Pte du Stiff

0   5 km

THE "ABER" REGION

L É O N

ABER-WRAC'H
ABER-BENOIT
ABER-ILDUT

POINTE DE CORSEN

POINTE SAINT-MATHIEU

Trémazan
Porspoder
Larret
Plouguerneau
Lannilis
St-Jaoua
Lampaul-Ploudalmézeau
Plouarzel
Gouesnou
Plabennec
Le Conquet
BREST
Saint-Renan
LANDERNEAU
Pencran
LA ROCHE-MAURICE
Dirinon
Le Folgoët
Lesneven
Landivisiau
Bodilis
Kerjean
Lambader

Brigognan
Plouescat
Batz
Roscoff
Saint-Pol-de-Léon
Carantec
Locquénolé
Plouézoc'h
Lanmeur

POINTE DE PRIMEL
Plougasnou
Saint-Jean-du-Doigt
Locquirec
BEG-AN-FRI
Plestin-les-Grèves

TRÉGOR

MORLAIX
N. 12
GUERLESQUIN

BERVEN
SAINT-SERVAIS
SAINT-THÉGONNEC
PLOUGONVEN
LE RELECQ
Roc'h ar Feuntenn
LAMPAUL-GUIMILIAU
GUIMILIAU
Locmélar
LA MARTYRE
COMMANA
Roc'h Trédudon
Roc'h Trévezel
SIZUN
Signal de Toussaines
MONTS D'ARRÉE
Pen ar Hoat
Saint-Rivoal
Brennilis
Huelgoat
Poullaouen
N. 787
PLOUGASTEL-DAOULAS
DAOULAS
Brasparts
St-Herbot
Carhaix-Plouguer

PENINSULA CROZON
Camaret
Kerlivit
LANDEVENNEC
Le Faou
Lopérec
Le Cloître-Pleyben
NANTES-BREST CANAL

POINTE DE PEN-HIR TAS-DE-POIS
POINTE DE DINAN
Crozon
Morgat
ARGOL
Menez Hom
Châteaulin
PLEYBEN
Châteauneuf-du-Faou
CLEDEN-POHER

CAP DE LA CHÈVRE
Ste-Anne-la-Palud
Cast
Roche du Feu
Trévarez
Laz
Saint-Goazec
Castel Ruffel
Toull Laeron
MONTAGNES NOIRES
Gourin

MORBIHAN

POINTE DU VAN
POINTE DU RAZ
Sein
CAP SIZUN
Douarnenez
LOCRONAN
Briec
Edern
Aulne
Odet

Pont-Croix
Meilars
Audierne
Plozévet

CORNOUAILLE

Guengat
Ergué-Gaberic
Elliant
St-Yvy
Scaër
Le Faouët

Plogastel-Saint-Germain
Aerodrome
QUIMPER
Rosporden
Bannalec
Locunolé
Arzano
Quimperlé

BIGOUDEN REGION
Tréguennec
Pont-L'Abbé
Bénodet
Fouesnant
Beg-Meil
CONCARNEAU
Pont-Aven
N. 165

N.D. DE TRONOEN
Loctudy
Le Guilvinec
Penmarc'h

POINTE DE TRÉVIGNON
Moëlan
Le Pouldu

Glénan

ATLANTIC OCEAN

Religious building (church, chapel, etc.)

Hills, observation platforms

Parish closes or main calvaries

Monastery, abbey

Vernacular building

Woodland

0   5   10   15   20KM

Designed by Michel Renouard
Drawn by Patrick Mérienne

In the Baie de Morlaix.

Cet ouvrage a été imprimé par Mame à Tours - La photocomposition est de Sécoprim à Saint-Grégoire (35) - La couverture a été imprimée par l'imprimerie Raynard à La Guerche-de-Bretagne et pelliculée par D.C.P. à Château-Gontier - Maquette et mise en pages : Marcel Oger du studio des Editions Ouest-France à Rennes - Prix à la parution en France continentale : 54 francs français.

1988 - OUEST-FRANCE - I.S.B.N. 2.7373.0141.6 - Dépôt légal : juin 1988 - N° éditeur 1466.01.05.06.88